TUDOR AND STUART COLCHESTER

by

Nigel Goose and Janet Cooper

An extract from

**THE VICTORIA HISTORY OF THE COUNTY OF ESSEX
VOLUME IX: THE BOROUGH OF COLCHESTER**
edited by Janet Cooper

Originally published in 1994 by Oxford University Press
for the University of London Institute of Historical Research

Reprinted 1998 by The Victoria History of the County of Essex
70 Duke Street, Chelmsford CM1 1JP

ISBN 0 86025 302 3

Published by
Victoria County History of Essex
70 Duke Street, Chelmsford, Essex CM1 1JP

Distributed by
Ian Henry Publications, Ltd
20 Park Drive, Romford, Essex RM1 4LH

Printed by
Interprint, Ltd., Malta

CONTENTS

MAIDENBURGH STREET IN THE 1890S

ILLUSTRATIONS

[Those marked with an asterisk (*) were not part of the original volume]

*The arrival of Marie de Medici in Colchester, 1638. Photograph in Colchester Museum of a 19th-century copy of a contemporary engraving

Maidenburgh Street in the 1890s. Watercolour painting by J. E. Bale at Colchester Museum

Map of Colchester c. 1500. Drawn by Pamela Studd from a draft by Janet Cooper

Map of the Siege of Colchester, 1648. From a broadsheet in the library of the Society of Antiquaries, London

*Details of a Prospect of Colchester from the north, 1697. Redrawn from a prospect by James Maheux in the British Library, Map 2390 (2)

Further details of a Prospect of Colchester from the north, 1697

Hythe Hill, 1887. Watercolour painting by J. E. Bale at Colchester Museum

*Part of the charter of Charles II to the borough. Charter in possession of Colchester Borough Council

*Portrait of Charles I from his charter to the borough. Charter in possession of Colchester Borough Council

*Portrait of Elizabeth I from her charter to the borough. Charter in possession of Colchester Borough Council

*Court roll, Hokeday Lawhundred, 1548. (Colchester Borough Muniments, deposited in Essex Record Office, D/B 5 Cr116)

*Assembly Book showing names of officers removed in January 1660. (Colchester Borough Muniments, E.R.O., D/B 5 Gb4, f. 208v.)

*Placard worn by a man punished in the tumbrel, 1583. (Colchester Borough Muniments, E.R.O. Acc. C1, uncat.)

*William Gilbert or Gilberd (d. 1603). Portrait in Colchester Museum

*Sir Harbottle Grimston, bart. (d. 1685). Engraving in E.R.O. Mint Portraits

*Sir Thomas Lucas of St. John's Abbey (d. 1611). Portrait in Colchester Museum

*Sir Charles Lucas (executed 1648). Portrait in Colchester Museum

*Bourne Mill in 1892. Photograph in Essex County Libraries, Colchester

*Tymperleys c. 1890. Photograph in Essex County Libraries, Colchester

*Colchester Bay Seal 1618. Photograph, Museum of London

*Colchester from Speed's Map of Essex, published in 1610. From a copy in E.R.O.

*Pargetting on no. 37 North Hill. Drawing by Richard Shackle

Headgate House, formerly the King's Head inn. Photograph by Alison Colchester 1993

*The 'Siege House', *c.* 1910. Photograph in Colchester Museum

The Red Lion inn. Photograph by Alison Colchester, 1993

North Hill, 1951. Photograph by E. Tattersall (RCHME Crown copyright)

*The burning of John Laurence at Colchester, 1555. Engraving in Colchester Museum

*Detail from court roll, 1547/8 (Colchester Borough Muniments, E.R.O., D/B 5 Cr116)

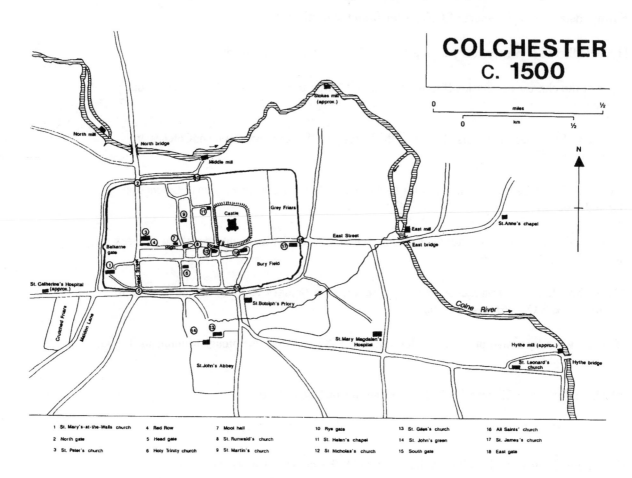

COLCHESTER
C. 1500

1 St. Mary's-at-the-Walls church	4 Red Row	7 Moot hall	10 Rye gate	13 St. Giles's church	16 All Saints' church
2 North gate	5 Head gate	8 St. Runwald's church	11 St. Helen's chapel	14 St. John's green	17 St. James's church
3 St. Peter's church	6 Holy Trinity church	9 St. Martin's church	12 St Nicholas's church	15 South gate	18 East gate

HYTHE HILL, 1887
with the tower of St. Leonard's church

The history of Tudor and Stuart Colchester forms a chapter in *The Victoria History of the Counties of England: Essex,* volume IX, *The Borough of Colchester* (1994), and is reproduced with the sanction and co-operation of the General Editor of the Victoria County History, Dr. C. R. J. Currie. The volume on the Borough of Colchester falls into two parts: I a chronological history incorporating the major themes, such as economic history, local government, and topographical development; II detailed sections on subsidiary topics including communications, the port, the castle, the fishery, markets and fairs, public services, churches, and education. The main section here reproduced forms the chapter on Tudor and Stuart Colchester in Part I and gives a general account of the development of the borough from *c.* 1500 to 1714; the appendix reproduces the list of bailiffs (to 1634/5) and mayors (from 1635/6 to 1714) from Part II. For detailed coverage of other subsidiary topics, and for an explanation of some of the abbreviations used in the footnotes, the reader is referred to the original edition of *V.C.H. Essex,* vol. IX. The pagination of the original edition has been retained, as have the cross references to other parts of the volume.

The area covered by the history of the Borough of Colchester in *V.C.H. Essex,* vol. IX, was that of the historic borough as it was from the Middle Ages until 1974. The Tudor and Stuart Colchester chapter thus deals with the ancient town centre, and with events in Berechurch, Greenstead, Lexden, and Mile End, and takes no account of the large area brought into the borough in 1974.

The architectural descriptions were compiled or revised by A. P. Baggs, the Architectural Editor of the Victoria History of the Counties of England. The account of Religious Life was written by Dr. C. C. Thornton. Dr. M. Byford and Mr. J. Walter commented on early drafts of the chapter when it was originally written; their help and that of the staffs of the Essex Record Office, particularly the Colchester branch, of the Local Studies Section of Essex County Libraries, and of the Colchester Museum, is gratefully acknowledged.

This reprint was prepared with the help of a generous grant from the Hervey Benham Charitable Trust.

TUDOR AND STUART COLCHESTER

THE earlier 16th century was a period of contraction in Colchester as the cloth trade, on which the town's economy depended, declined. The borough began to recover about the middle of the century, and its economy was greatly boosted from 1565 by the arrival of Dutch immigrants who introduced the manufacture of new draperies, the lightweight bays and says which were the mainstay of Colchester's cloth industry throughout the 17th century, and the foundation of its prosperity and growth.[1] The town was also known for its oysters and for its candied eryngo or sea holly, a sweetmeat and reputed aphrodisiac; both were presented to important visitors and sent to the borough's patrons and friends at court. Borough government was reorganized by Charles I's charter of 1635 which, among other provisions, gave the town a mayor in place of the two bailiffs who had hitherto been its chief officers.[2]

Colchester's population, declining from the mid 15th century, may have continued to contract in the early 16th.[3] Estimates based on the subsidy returns of 1524–5 suggest a figure in the range of 3,500–5,000, with one of c. 4,000 probably closest to the truth.[4] That figure is consistent with another estimate, based on the numbers taking the oath of allegiance to the heirs of Henry VIII and Anne Boleyn, of c. 3,600 (excluding clergy) in 1534, at a time when the town's population may have reached its nadir. From then on there are signs of slow recovery, the population reaching c. 4,600, including 431 Dutch immigrants, in the 1570s. Thereafter the trend was distinctly upward, despite short-lived interruptions in the early 1590s and between 1606 and 1610, producing a total of c. 11,000 by the 1620s, including 1,535 Dutch. An estimate of 10,400 for 1674 suggests only slight contraction by that date, despite the ravages of the siege of 1648 and the great plague of 1665–6. Thereafter numbers seem to have at best stagnated and by the mid 18th century Colchester, with c. 2,342 households,[5] was falling well behind other more rapidly developing towns.

Part of the town's growth was due to natural increase, a surplus of births over deaths, despite the appearance of small deficits in both the 1590s and the 1620s, and another larger shortfall during the quinquennium 1601–5 caused mainly by the severe plague epidemic of 1603–4.[6] Although births did outnumber deaths over the period 1561–1640 as a whole, the surplus is insufficient to account for the extent of the expansion achieved. Immigration, from elsewhere in England and from overseas, played an essential part in the growth, a feature of the town's development that was of great concern to the urban authorities in the later 16th and early 17th century.[7]

Colchester's growth was punctuated by outbreaks of epidemic disease. The years 1514, 1545, 1557–9, 1569–70, 1586–8, 1597, 1603–4, 1625–6, 1631, 1651, 1665–6,

[1] *Immigrants and Minorities*, i. 263–80; L. Roker, 'Flemish and Dutch Community in Colch. in the 16th and 17th Cent.' (Lond. Univ. M.A. thesis, 1963); *Reg. of Baptisms in Dutch Ch. in Colch.* ed. W. J. C. Moens, (Huguenot Soc. xii).
[2] *Diary of John Evelyn*, ed. W. Bray, i. 314–15; *O.E.D.* s.v. eryngo; E.R.O., D/B 5 Aa1/1–26; Aa1/35, ff. 1–90.
[3] The following paragraphs are based on N. Goose,

'Economic and Social Aspects of Provincial Towns: a comparative study of Cambridge, Colchester, and Reading c. 1500–1700' (Camb. Univ. Ph.D. thesis, 1984), 248–51.
[4] Cf. Britnell, *Growth and Decline*, 201–2.
[5] Morant, *Colch.* 107–36; the figure excludes Mile End and Berechurch.
[6] Goose, 'Econ. and Social Aspects', 263–7.
[7] Below, this chapter, Soc. Structure.

and 1679 had particularly high mortality.[8] The high mortality of 1557–9 was probably caused by the national epidemic of influenza and typhus in those years,[9] while that of 1597 was possibly due to either famine or disease induced by malnutrition, the result of four successive years of high grain prices.[10] Plague appears to have been responsible for most of the other years of high death rate, and was active in the town at other times, producing peaks of mortality in particular parishes. St. Botolph's, for instance, experienced additional years of high mortality in 1578, 1583, and 1610–11, St. James's in 1580, Lexden in 1595, and St. Leonard's in 1638–9. The frequency with which the poor parish of St. Botolph experienced such crises demonstrates the close relationship between poverty and epidemic disease.[11] None of the epidemics was capable of stemming the town's growth. Although plague was a frequent visitor to the town, only in 1597, 1603–4, and 1625–6 did mortality reach double the average level for a sample of parishes representing the town as a whole, and under 10 per cent of total mortality in the early 17th century was due to the additional deaths that such crises produced.

The plague of 1665–6 was of a completely different order of magnitude. The death toll was variously given as 5,259 for the 17 months between August 1665 and December 1666, of which 4,731 were from plague, and 5,034 for the 67 weeks from 8 September 1665 to 21 December 1666, of which 4,526 were from plague.[12] Approximately half the town's population perished in the epidemic, probably making it the most destructive outbreak experienced by any large town in early modern England. The full resources of the corporation were mobilized. Two new pest houses were built, in St. Mary's-at-the-Walls and at Mile End, while searchers and bearers of the dead were appointed to dispose of the bodies.[13] Funds collected in Colchester churches quickly proved inadequate to relieve the sufferers, and were supplemented by a tax on villages within 5 miles of the town, authorized by the J.P.s and producing £217 a month. Early in 1666 an additional £250 a month for three months was ordered to be levied in the hundreds of Lexden, Dunmow, and Hinckford, and by July funds were also being raised in the hundreds of Clavering, Uttlesford, and Ongar, and in Witham half hundred. In May 1666 weekly collections were made in London churches by order of Charles II, amassing a total of £1,307 10s. In all c. £2,700 was raised in taxes and donations for the relief of the town, a sum that was administered with painstaking diligence by the corporation and its officials, despite the absence of the mayor and several aldermen, assistants, and councillors during October and November 1666.[14] A surplus of £400 of the money collected for the poor remained in the corporation's coffers some 18 years later.[15]

The immediate impact of the epidemic was profound, but both the population and the economy recovered surprisingly rapidly. Already in March 1666, when the months of peak mortality were still to come, 279 houses stood empty. By 1674, however, only 63 houses were empty, showing that Colchester had conformed to the typical pattern whereby urban population losses were quickly made good by an influx of migrants.[16] Cloth production also quickly recovered, and achieved new heights as early as 1668.[17]

Disturbances, some politically as well as economically motivated, marked mid

[8] Goose, 'Econ. and Social Aspects', 300–21; E.A.T. 3rd ser. iv. 134–45.

[9] Econ. H.R. xviii. 120–9; xlvi. 291–4.

[10] Below, this chapter, Soc. Structure.

[11] P. Slack, Impact of Plague in Tudor and Stuart Eng. 112, 116, 124–6.

[12] B.L. Stowe MS. 840, ff. 44–5; E.R.O., D/P 200/1/6 (unfoliated), following baptisms.

[13] E.R.O., D/B 5 Aa1/23; D/B 5 R1, f. 217.

[14] E.R.O., D/B 5 Gb4, ff. 315v.–346v., 356; P.R.O., PC 2/59, pp. 5–6; Cal. S.P. Dom. 1665–6, 398; E.A.T. 3rd ser. iv. 141–2.

[15] Cal. S.P. Dom. 1683–4, 258.

[16] P.R.O., E 179/246/22; E.A.T. 3rd ser. iv. 145; Medical Hist. xix. 333–41; Crisis and Order in Eng. Towns 1500–1700, ed. P. Clark and P. Slack, 170; J. Patten, Eng. Towns, 132.

[17] Below, this chapter, Econ.

DECORATIVE DETAILS FROM THE COURT ROLL FOR 1547/8

and later 16th-century Colchester.[18] A few attracted the attention of the government in London. A Norfolk priest spread rumours of Kett's rebellion in the town in 1549, and two Colchester men were pardoned for 'treason and insurrection' that year. On 31 August another six men, presumably rebels but not, apparently, from Colchester, were condemned by the earl of Oxford and Sir Thomas Darcy and hanged at the town gates and in the market place.[19] Jerome Gilberd, a lawyer who was to be recorder of the town in the first year of Mary's reign, seems to have been suspected in 1550 of writing two seditious bills,[20] and in 1563 a shearman was accused of repeating 'slanderous reports' of the queen.[21] Between 1577 and 1579 Robert Mantell or Blosse, a seaman who had claimed at Maldon to be Edward VI, was imprisoned in Colchester castle.[22] While there Mantell built up a following in the town which included the councillor Stephen Holt, who with the gaoler and his assistant was suspected of aiding his escape in July 1579.[23] Mantell was recaptured, imprisoned in Newgate, and executed in 1581.[24] In 1584 Thomas Debell, a servant of Catherine Audley of Berechurch and like his mistress a suspected popish recusant, was imprisoned by the bailiffs for 'very dangerous' speeches pointing out that Mary Queen of Scots was the next heir to the throne and complaining that Mantell had been executed on the evidence of only one instead of two witnesses. The town clerk and the Privy Council took a less serious view of the matter, and Debell seems to have been released.[25]

In 1588 the borough supplied a ship and perhaps a pinnace for service against the Armada, and in April that year sailors from as far down the Colne as Brightlingsea were ordered to appear at the moot hall, presumably so that crews could be found.[26] Apart from the Civil War, national affairs did not impinge on Colchester again until the 1680s. In 1683, while the assembly of mayor, aldermen, and assistants duly presented a loyal address to Charles II on the discovery of the Popish plot, other burgesses were feared to be 'dangerous to the peace and government' of the country, and a drunken townsman boasted that he had fought against the old king and would fight against the present one if necessary.[27] The earl of Oxford's regiment was stationed in the town for about a month during Monmouth's rebellion in the summer of 1685.[28] In December 1688 the assembly ordered the distribution of arms to some burgesses, and troops were again quartered in the town.[29] In 1691 the recorder and the M.P., Sir Isaac Rebow, examined some 'very dangerous persons' who had been trying to escape overseas.[30]

Royal and other important visits to the town were few, but generally costly. When Catherine of Aragon came to Colchester in 1515 on her way to Walsingham (Norf.) she was given a purse and £10.[31] In 1544 the bailiffs were ordered to prepare provisions for 1,600–2,000 horse accompanying Henry VIII to Harwich.[32] Colchester declared for Mary at her accession on 19 July, and the queen travelled through the town on 26 July 1553, on her way from Framlingham to London. The streets were mended in preparation for her visit, and she was presented with a

[18] Below, this chapter, Soc. Structure.
[19] Cal. Pat. 1549–51, 2; B.L. Stowe MS. 829, f. 32; Rebellion, Popular Protest, and the Social Order in Early Modern Eng. ed. P. Slack, 52, 71.
[20] Acts of P.C. 1550–2, 138, 159; E.R.O., D/B 5 Cr120, rot. 1.
[21] E.R.O., D/B 5 Sb2/1, f. 22v.
[22] Cal. Assize Rec. Essex, Eliz. I, p. 175.
[23] E.R.O., D/Y 2/6, p. 13; D/Y 2/8, p. 207; Acts of P.C. 1580–1, 29.
[24] Cal. Assize Rec. Essex, Eliz. I, p. 215.
[25] E.R.O., D/B5 Sb2/4, ff. 36v.–37; D/Y 2/7, p. 199; D/Y

2/8, pp. 319, 323; B.L. Stowe MS. 150, f. 33.
[26] E.R.O., D/B 5 Gb1, 6, 15 April, 1588; D/Y 2/3, p. 53; V.C.H. Essex, ii. 221.
[27] E.R.O., D/B 5 Gb5, f. 207; D/B 5 Sb2/9, f. 319 and v.; Cal. S.P. Dom. 1683, 89.
[28] William Holcroft His Book, ed. J. A. Sharpe, pp. vi, 33, 49.
[29] E.R.O., D/B 5 Gb5, ff. 308–9.
[30] Cal. S.P. Dom. 1690–1, 252.
[31] E.R.O., D/B 5 R1, f. 118.
[32] S. Dale, Hist. and Antiq. Harwich, 249; E.R.O., D/Y 2/9, p. 355.

silver gilt cup and cover and £20.[33] Elizabeth I spent two or three days in Colchester in 1561; she was presumably met by the bailiffs, aldermen, and councillors in their livery gowns, welcomed by the recorder, and presented with a silver gilt cup and £20, as was planned for cancelled visits in 1578 and 1579. When the duke of York, later James II, visited the town in 1667 he was presented only with a box of candied eryngo, and a similar present was given to his son-in-law the future William III in 1681.[34] An expensive entertainment was planned for William on his journey to Harwich and the Netherlands in 1691, but on the return journey he was merely offered an oyster.[35] The duke of Marlborough visited Colchester in 1704, but his entertainment apparently cost only £2.[36]

Although it was overshadowed in the region by Ipswich, Colchester was by far the largest town in Essex,[37] and its castle housed the county gaol until 1666. The county town, however, was Chelmsford, where both the assizes and the county quarter sessions were usually held. Colchester acquired none of the legal and other business which those courts generated; it had fewer inns than the much smaller Chelmsford, and seems to have attracted fewer lawyers.[38] Nevertheless a number of professional men settled in Colchester, some in pursuit of their careers, others in retirement. Thomas Audley, a lawyer from Earls Colne who moved to Colchester as town clerk in 1514 and ended a career in the royal service as Lord Chancellor and Baron Audley of Walden,[39] was perhaps the town's most distinguished burgess. Although he resigned as town clerk in 1531 he had by then settled at Berechurch within the liberty, and retained his links with the town until his death in 1544.[40] Francis Jobson, son and grandson of Colchester bailiffs, also made a career in the royal service, becoming lieutenant of the Tower of London in 1564, and acquiring former monastic lands including West Donyland with its house at Monkwick, within the liberty. He married Elizabeth, daughter of Arthur Plantagenet, Viscount Lisle, thus connecting himself with her half brother John Dudley, later duke of Northumberland, father of Lady Jane Grey. He served as M.P. for Colchester in 1552, in 1553–4, and 1555.[41]

Samuel Halsnoth or Harsnett (d. 1631), son of a Colchester baker William Halsnoth, obtained his degree at Cambridge and returned to the town briefly as master of the grammar school 1587–8. He ended his career as archbishop of York; although he had not lived there since 1588 he left his library to the borough.[42] His cousin Adam Harsnett followed him to Cambridge where he took his B.D. in 1612; he was later known as a moderate Puritan theologian.[43] William Gilbert or Gilberd (d. 1603), son of Jerome Gilberd, also went from Colchester to Cambridge. He became physician to Elizabeth I and James I, but his reputation rests chiefly on his pioneering study of magnetism, *De Magnete* (1600).[44] Thomas Skinner, physician and biographer of General George Monk, duke of Albemarle, practised in Colchester where he died in 1679.[45] The madrigal

[33] E.R.O., D/Y 2/2, pp. 29, 31–3.
[34] *E.J.* xxiii. 66–7.
[35] E.R.O., D/B 5 Gb5, ff. 337, 348.
[36] Ibid. D/B 5 Ab 1/24.
[37] W. J. Petchey, *Prospect of Maldon*, 10, 12.
[38] Ibid. 138; H. Grieve, *Sleepers and Shadows*, vol. ii, chapter 1 (forthcoming).
[39] E.R.O., D/B 5 Cr86, rott. 1, 2d.; *Complete Peerage*, i.

348–9.
[40] *E.A.T.* 3rd ser. xv. 86–7; below, Outlying Parts (West Donyland, Manors).
[41] *D.N.B.*; *Lisle Letters*, ed. M. St. Clair Byrne, vi, p. 280; Morant, *Colch.* 104, 137.
[42] *D.N.B*; below, Soc. and Cultural (Libraries).
[43] *D.N.B.* [44] Ibid.; Morant, *Colch.* App. p. 20.
[45] Morant, *Colch.* 118.

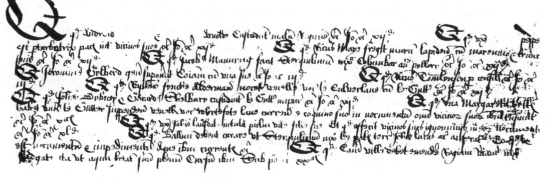

HEADING FOR THE HOKEDAY LAWHUNDRED, 1548
the record of an important meeting of the borough court on 23 April, 1548

composer John Wilbye lived in retirement at Colchester from *c.* 1628 until his death in 1638, as a member of the household of Mary Darcy, Countess Rivers, daughter of his earlier patron Sir Thomas Kitson of Hengrave (Suff.).[46]

The Civil War

Growing religious differences between opponents and followers of Archbishop Laud fuelled factionalism in borough government and may have led to the arrest and trial of John Bastwick, later a leading parliamentarian writer, in 1634.[47] Most borough officers in the 1630s favoured a presbyterian or independent form of church government, but Robert Buxton, mayor 1636–7 and 1645–6, supported Laud's reforms and may have had links with the court through his trade in candied eryngo.[48] In January 1642 the town petitioned parliament against bishops, chancellors, and archdeacons and their ceremonies, as well as against 'idle, double-faced, scandalous, and ignorant ministers', probably a reference to the hated Thomas Newcomen, Laudian rector of Holy Trinity church.[49] The town defended itself in the courts against the extension of the forest bounds in the 1630s.[50] It seems to have paid the £400 assessed for ship money in 1635 and 1636 although both payments, like others from the county, were late, but in 1638 it refused to pay, and in 1639 petitioned for a reduction in its assessment.[51]

The first violence, in June 1640, was directed against the recusant Anne, wife of Sir Henry Audley of Berechurch, and its underlying cause may have been as much the distress resulting from a decline in the cloth industry and resentment against the billeting of soldiers in the town as fear of papist plots. When two strange Irishmen appeared in the town at the end of May the rumour spread that Lady Audley, or her fellow recusant Bestney Barker at Monkwick, was gathering armed papists, apparently led by the archbishop of Canterbury and the bishop of Ely, and even that the queen's mother, Marie de Medici, was expected there. A group of apprentices and other young men led by a drum marched from the town to the Hythe intending to go to Berechurch and Monkwick, but most were stopped by the borough constables before they reached either house.[52] The following year a papist's house in the town was searched for weapons and for letters from Ireland.[53]

Violence in 1642 was directed against the Lucas family at St. John's Abbey. They and the burgesses had been in dispute throughout the 1630s over the inclosure of common lands and over the damage caused by the pipes of the town waterworks.[54] Sir John Lucas's entertainment of Marie de Medici on her way from Harwich to London in 1638 may also have been unpopular.[55] Early in 1640 there was a further dispute, over the activities of saltpetremen who, Sir John alleged, had done considerable damage to St. John's Abbey but had not even visited other houses in the town.[56] In 1641 Sir John infringed the borough liberties by prosecuting those involved in an inclosure riot at Rovers Tye in the House of Lords instead of in the borough court.[57] In June 1642 he seems to have been suspected of stockpiling

[46] D. Brown, *Wilbye*, 9, 53; *Complete Peerage*, xi. 26.

[47] F. M. Condick, 'Life and Works of Dr. John Bastwick' (Lond. Univ. Ph.D. thesis, 1982), 61–79; below, this chapter, Boro. Govt.; Religious Life.

[48] *Colch. Hist. Studies*, ed. D. Stephenson, 6.

[49] *C.J.* ii. 387; *Petition of Inhabitants of Colch. to Parl.* (1642): copy in E.R.O.

[50] E.R.O., D/B 5 Gb3, ff. 164v., 167, 194.

[51] Ibid. f. 200; *Cal. S.P. Dom.* 1635–6, 435; 1637, 532; 1637–8, 419; Morant, *Colch.* 54.

[52] E.R.O., D/B 5 Sb2/7, ff. 277v.–278; P.R.O., SP 16/458/12, 13; *Rebellion, Popular Protest, and the Social Order in Early Modern Eng.* ed. Slack, 131–2.

[53] *Jnl. of Sir Simonds D'Ewes*, ed. W. H. Coates, 125.

[54] Below, Commons; Public Services.

[55] E.R.O., D/B 5 Gb3, f. 187; *Exact Catalogue of Essex Malignants* (1648): copy in E.C.L. Colch.

[56] P.R.O., SP 16/449, no. 25; SP 16/451, no. 25.

[57] Hist. MSS. Com. 3, *4th Rep. H. L.* p. 86; *L.J.* iv. 307; *Jnl. of Peasant Studies*, ii. 133–58.

arms and ammunition.[58] When, at the end of August, his plans to join Charles I became known, a drum was beaten and a crowd said to be several thousand strong assembled and broke into St. John's Abbey, where they seized arms and armour as well as household goods. They went on to attack the Lucas tombs in St. Giles's church. Sir John and his family and Thomas Newcomen, who had been going to accompany Sir John, were taken and imprisoned in the moot hall. Lucas and Newcomen were removed safely to London only by the intervention of two M.P.s, Sir Thomas Barrington and Harbottle Grimston.[59] The crowd went on to attack Sir Henry Audley's house at Berechurch and then that of Countess Rivers at St. Osyth before moving further afield.[60]

In August 1642 the county committee thanked Colchester for its zeal in raising money and plate and in offering horses for the army.[61] By October that year the trained band under John Langley was at Brentwood on its way to London, and the town was being asked for £285 10s. to pay its troops, as well as for horses for dragoons. The money was still unpaid in November, and the soldiers were becoming discontented.[62] That month Harbottle Grimston urged the mayor to fortify the town against an expected royalist attack, and Henry Barrington was given command of the town's ordnance.[63] Early in 1643 Colchester sent a company of troops to Cambridge, but in March it was 54 men short and its pay in arrears.[64] Requests for men and money were repeated in July and September, by which time the company was only 20 men short.[65] In October the borough tried unsuccessfully to have the trained band recalled to defend Colchester from the enemy or from its own 'unruly multitude'.[66] In December the band was still short 33 properly equipped men, and three months' assessment was unpaid.[67] Almost all the leading burgesses subscribed to the earl of Essex's army in June 1643.[68]

A Colchester committee for the sequestration of delinquents, composed of the mayor, the recorder Harbottle Grimston, and alderman Henry Barrington, was set up in March 1643, and a similar, although slightly larger, committee for the defence of the Eastern Association in September that year.[69] In July that year representatives of the county gentry and some inhabitants of Colchester petitioned parliament for the appointment of an M.P. as governor of the town.[70]

In 1642 or 1643 Grimston's relations with the town deteriorated as many leading burgesses moved away from the presbyterianism he supported towards more extreme forms of protestantism. There may also have been rumours that he had been profiteering at a time when the townsmen were suffering from the collapse of the cloth trade. Grimston alleged he was 'traduced and libelled', not only by the poor but also by many of the better sort.[71] Some opposition to parliament seems to have appeared in 1643, when the county committee complained of the slow collection of rates, and a man at the Hythe grumbled that parliament would not listen to the king.[72] In June the mayor was warned to take care to prevent disorders and riots at the coming midsummer fair.[73] In 1644 Colchester failed to

[58] C.J. ii. 615.
[59] Hist. MSS. Com. 9, 10th Rep. App. VI, Bray, pp. 146–7; Mercurius Rusticus or the Countries Complaint (1723), 1–6; C.J. ii. 732, 736, 882.
[60] Mercurius Rusticus, 13–15, 37; Cal. S.P. Dom. 1641–3, 377; E.R.O., D/B 5 Sb2/7, ff. 300v.–303; V.C.H. Essex, ii. 231.
[61] B.L. Stowe MS. 189, f. 5.
[62] E.R.O., D/Y 2/8, pp. 39, 173, 177–8; Morant, Colch. 55.
[63] E.R.O., D/Y 2/8, pp. 44–5; D/B 5 Gb3, f. 232v.
[64] Ibid. D/Y 2/7, p. 299; D/Y 2/9, pp. 81, 83, 87.

[65] Ibid. D/Y 2/8, p. 59; D/Y 2/9, pp. 107, 111, 115.
[66] B.L. Egerton MS. 2647, f. 361; ibid. Stowe MS. 189, f. 19.   [67] E.R.O., D/Y 2/9, p. 123.
[68] Ibid. D/Y 2/2, pp. 219–35; Colch. Hist. Studies, ed. Stephenson, 5, 13.
[69] Acts and Ordinances of the Interregnum, ed. C. H. Firth and R. S. Rait, i. 112, 292–3.   [70] C.J. iii. 184.
[71] E.R.O., D/Y 2/8, p. 67; A. Fletcher, Outbreak of Eng. Civil War, 294.
[72] B.L. Stowe MS. 189, f. 12; E.R.O., D/Y 2/8, p. 158.
[73] L.J. vi. 102.

SIR HARBOTTLE GRIMSTON, BART.
High Steward and M.P. for the borough

WILLIAM GILBERT
OR GILBERD
physician and scientist

impress enough soldiers for the earl of Manchester's army, and the same year the borough petitioned parliament for relief from its heavy weekly assessment.[74] The petition seems to have had little effect, for in 1645 the total collected rose from £4,406 to £6,280. In all, between the start of the civil war in 1642 and Michaelmas 1648 the town contributed £30,177.[75] In addition, voluntary collections were made, such as those for shoes for the earl of Essex's soldiers in 1644 and for the garrison of Gloucester in 1645.[76]

A parliamentarian writer accused Robert Harmer, town lecturer 1640–8, of stirring up the people against the 'heretics and schismatics' of the army, and the townsmen of abusing the soldiers quartered on them.[77] In January 1648 some townsmen did refuse to accept soldiers billeted on them.[78] After a 'riotous and tumultuous' assembly on 30 April 1648 the trained band was called out to keep the peace on May Day. Two days later the county band had to be ordered to suppress the 'tumult' in the town, which parliament no doubt feared was related to similar risings in Suffolk, notably at Bury St. Edmunds.[79] Shortly afterwards a disgruntled townsman expressed the hope that now the troopers were gone he would have some of the best beer, and even 'a day to plunder the roundheads and the Independents'.[80]

The election of the moderate John Shaw as mayor in September 1647 suggests that opinion, at least among the free burgesses, was swinging against the army, and Shaw's removal by the army presumably added to its unpopularity. When a royalist force of c. 5,600 under George Goring, earl of Norwich, commonly known as Lord Goring, approached the town on 12 June 1648 the gates were shut against them, but were opened after a brief skirmish. The royalists, whose officers included Sir Charles Lucas, younger brother of Sir John, seem to have been searching for supplies and men and intended to stay in Colchester only a few days.[81] On 13 June, however, a pursuing parliamentarian force under Thomas Fairfax, Lord Fairfax, reached Colchester, and having failed to defeat the royalists in a skirmish around Head gate settled down to besiege the town.

The siege lasted until 28 August and caused serious physical damage to the town and temporary disruption to its trade.[82] The town was unprepared, and although at first the royalists managed to bring in food and ammunition from the Hythe and from the countryside north-east of the town, the completion of encircling siege works in mid July cut them off from further supplies. In the almost nightly sallies and skirmishes in June and early July both sides burnt or pulled down houses outside the wall. Grimston's house at Crutched Friars was at first occupied by the royalists but taken by the besiegers at the end of June. St. John's Abbey was held by the royalists until it was successfully stormed in mid July; having plundered the house the parliamentarian troops broke into the Lucas family vault in St. Giles's church and dismembered the bodies there.[83] The burgesses' request to Fairfax

74 B.L. Stowe MS. 189, f. 25; E.R.O., D/B 5 Gb3, f. 245v.
75 Morant, Colch. 56.
76 E.R.O., D/B 5 Gb3, ff. 246, 253v.
77 True Relation of the Taking of Colch. (1648): copy in E.C.L. Colch.
78 B.L. Stowe MS. 842, ff. 10–12.
79 Ibid. f. 14; C.J. v. 550; Diary of Ralph Josselin, ed. A. Macfarlane, 124; V.C.H. Suff. ii. 192.
80 E.R.O., D/B 5 Sb2/9, f. 17.
81 Matthew Carter, True Relation of the Expedition of Kent, Essex, and Colch. 1648, 59; Exact Narrative of Every Day's Proceedings since the Insurrection in Essex, 4–5: copy in E.C.L. Colch.; J. Rushworth, Hist. Colln. ii. 1160; Diary of Ralph

Josselin, 128; Colchester's Tears (1648), 12–13; B. P. Lyndon, 'Second Civil War in Essex' (TS. in E.R.O.), 2–3; cf. Hist. MSS. Com. 27, 12th Rep. IX, Beaufort, pp. 22–3; Hist. MSS. Com. 17, 14th Rep. App. IX, pp. 281–2; Colch. Hist. Studies, 8.
82 Morant, Colch. 58–69; Carter, True Relation, 59–94; Hist. MSS. Com. 17, 14th Rep. App. IX, 281–90; Diary and Plan of Siege of Colch.: copy in E.C.L. Colch.; Lyndon, 'Second Civil War in Essex', 1– 297.
83 Last News from Colch. (1648); Great and Bloody Fight at Colch. (1648); Letter to Wm. Lenthall of Late Fight at Colch. (1648): copies in E.C.L. Colch.; Carter, True Relation of the Expedition, 71; Hist. MSS. Com. 27, 12th Rep. IX, Beaufort, p. 28.

FIG. 8

SIR THOMAS LUCAS
owner of St. John's Abbey

SIR CHARLES LUCAS
Royalist leader at the siege of Colchester

early in the siege that they might continue exporting bays was not surprisingly refused, as was their request on 7 August that non-combatants be allowed to leave the town. Both sides were accused of plundering and even killing townspeople, and the townspeople, particularly the poorer ones, suffered severely as the town was starved into submission. By the end of July the besieged were reduced to eating horsemeat, and by the end of the siege dogs and cats had also been consumed. The poor diet and the lack of water after the besiegers had cut the town's water-pipes at the end of July, caused 'fluxes' from which some townsmen died.[84]

Sir Charles Lucas, who was blamed by the parliamentarians for bringing the royalist army to Colchester,[85] had apparently expected to be able to recruit from among the impoverished weavers there.[86] He and Goring may have expected some support from the borough assembly, and after the siege several borough officers, including three aldermen, suspected of royalist sympathies were removed. One of them, Robert Buxton, with 'one Leomans', probably Henry Leming, allegedly encouraged Goring to hold out in the early days of the siege.[87] On the other hand, a royalist officer recorded that during the siege the townspeople, their 'inveterate enemies', were always ready to help foment mutiny among the soldiers and that the mayor, William Cooke, refused to co-operate with Goring in the distribution of bread.[88] On 27 August the historian John Rushworth reported from Fairfax's camp that negotiations were going on both with the royalist delegation and with 'many of our people in town'.[89] Of those sequestered or fined after the siege only Henry Leming was from Colchester.[90] Parliament, however, blamed the townspeople for the siege. Fairfax, in refusing permission for the baymakers to carry on their trade, said they should have considered their trade before they let the royalists into the town,[91] and the committee of both houses, writing on 27 July 1648 to Yarmouth which was threatened by the royalist fleet, pointed out that Colchester was suffering grievously for being 'very forward to invite and receive the enemy'.[92]

On 27 August the royalists agreed to Fairfax's stern conditions for surrender. All soldiers and officers below the rank of captain were to have fair quarter; captains and above were to surrender at mercy. On Fairfax's orders Sir Charles Lucas and Sir George Lisle were executed at once, outside the castle, an unprecedented action taken to satisfy 'military justice' and to avenge the innocent blood which they had caused to be spilt.[93] Fairfax also imposed a fine of £12,000, £2,000 of which was later returned for the poor, on the town. Half the fine was paid by the Dutch congregation. Of the rest, £3,293 was collected in Head ward and North ward, no fewer than 17 individuals contributing £100 or more, and the remainder was presumably paid by South and East wards. Such contributions were exacted from those who had already suffered considerable losses; in 1654 a total of 19 inhabitants claimed to have lost almost £7,000 between them during the siege.[94]

The town remained suspect, and in October the mayor was warned of the many 'disaffected persons' who with others lately in arms had 'dangerous designs' in

[84] *True Relation of the Taking of Colch.* (1648); Rushworth, *Hist. Colln.* ii. 1242.

[85] *True Relation of the Taking of Colch.* (1648).

[86] Carter, *True Relation of the Expedition*, 59.

[87] *To Wm. Lenthall, Speaker of the Ho. of Commons* (1648), 4: copy in E.C.L. Colch.; *Colch. Hist. Studies*, 9; below, this chapter, Boro. Govt.

[88] Carter, *True Relation of the Expedition*, 67, 78.

[89] Bodl. MS. Tanner 57/1, f. 247.

[90] *Cal. Cttee. for Advance of Money*, 944, 1140.

[91] Hist. MSS. Com. 38, *14th Rep. App. IX, Round*, p. 285.

[92] *Cal. S.P. Dom.* 1648–9, 219.

[93] *Letter from Ld. Fairfax concerning Surrender of Colch.* (1648); *True Relation of the Taking of Colch.* (1648): copies in E.C.L. Colch.

[94] *Cal. Cttee. for Compounding*, 134, 141; *Reg. Dutch Ch. in Colch.* (Huguenot Soc. xii), 136; E.R.O., D/Y 2/2, pp. 243, 319; *E.J.* xviii. 39–47; P.R.O., SP 23/155, nos. 601–3; Morant, *Colch.* 73.

hand.[95] One man was accused in 1649 of saying that he wished all the roundheads were hanged, and the following year two Colchester men thought Cromwell a rogue.[96] There were fears in 1651 that royalists would seize Colchester for Charles II, then in Scotland. A drummer who spread prophecies of the overthrow of Cromwell may have reflected the mood of some poorer townsmen. A garrison of 300 men from the county trained bands was placed in the town, and after an initial delay the defences built during the earlier civil war and siege were destroyed.[97] During the early 1650s a party opposed to Henry Barrington and the 'Cromwellians' gained the upper hand in borough government, leading to a purge of the corporation in 1655.[98] Four Colchester men were arrested in connexion with the abortive 'Salisbury insurrection' of 1655. One of them, 'Capt. Barker', may have been Robert Barker of Monkwick.[99] Troops were quartered in the town in 1656 and 1657, and there was 'great talk of Cavalier attempts again',[1] but in June 1659 the town offered to raise a troop of horse for parliament.[2]

ECONOMIC HISTORY

The Early 16th-Century Economy

In the early 16th century Colchester ranked ninth among English provincial towns in terms of taxable wealth and seventh in terms of size of taxable population.[3] It had fared well compared to many other towns in the later Middle Ages; its high position in the urban rankings testifies to the vigour of its growth after the Black Death of 1348–9, as well as to its relatively gentle later decline. The town's early 16th-century economy exhibited a diversity typical of developed early modern towns which served as manufacturing centres and markets both for their immediate areas and for a wider hinterland, and also performed administrative functions. Most large towns also possessed an economic specialism, and Colchester's economy depended heavily upon its cloth industry, allied to its role as a port.

Diversity and specialization are both revealed in the town's occupational structure (Tables I and II). The number and range of occupations, c. 56 in the earlier 16th century and 102 in the 17th, mark Colchester off from the smaller towns of Essex. Its important market, held three times weekly, and its three annual fairs brought outsiders to the town and encouraged the growth of service industries, and the port attracted mariners and other transport workers. Nevertheless, as many as 47 per cent of the sample for the period 1500–79 were manufacturers, and the dominant group among them were producers of woollen cloth.

The fundamental importance of cloth production and trade to the town in the early 16th century is even more apparent from the distribution of wealth in 1524 and 1525,[4] when the occupations of 252 of the 996 individuals included in either of the two subsidy assessments are known.[5] Of the seven men with taxable wealth of £100 or more, four were clothiers, one was a merchant and clothier, one a merchant, and the other, John Christmas, had made his wealth in cloth and trade. Of those assessed at between £40 and £99, 11 were clothiers or merchants, 2 were

95 Cal. S.P. Dom. 1648–9, 307–8.
96 E.R.O., D/B 5 Sb2/9, ff. 26v., 39.
97 Ibid. f. 57; Cal. S.P. Dom. 1651, 90, 108, 185, 281.
98 Below, this chapter, Boro. Govt.
99 Cal. S.P. Dom. 1655, 367–8; V.C.H. Essex, ii. 239; below, Outlying Parts (W. Donyland, Manors).
1 Cal. S.P. Dom. 1656–7, 171; 1658–9, 123; Diary of

Ralph Josselin, 381.
2 C.J. vii. 698.
3 Goose, 'Econ. and Social Aspects', Tables 1.1 and 1.2, pp. 35, 37.
4 P.R.O., E 179/108/147, 162, 169.
5 Occupations identified mainly from wills and borough court rolls.

TABLE I: COLCHESTER OCCUPATIONAL STRUCTURE

| | 1500–79 | | 1580–1619 | | 1620–59 | | 1660–99 | |
	no.	per cent	no.	per cent	no.	per cent	no.	per cent
Textiles	65	26.5	104	26.4	194	37.1	82	40.0
Clothing	21	8.6	49	12.4	37	7.1	48	6.8
Leather (raw)	3.	1.2	5	1.3	6	1.1	8	1.1
Household	30	12.2	24	6.1	38	7.3	53	7.5
Tools and Arms	5	2.0	1	0.3	12	2.3	27	3.8
Housing	9	3.7	18	4.6	9	1.7	38	5.4
Food and Drink	29	11.8	52	13.2	60	11.5	81	11.5
Transport	28	11.4	45	11.4	42	8.0	45	6.4
Service	19	7.8	27	6.9	22	4.2	19	2.7
Education	–	–	2	0.5	1	0.2	5	0.7
Medicine	2	0.8	6	1.5	8	1.5	22	3.1
Miscellaneous	34	13.9	61	15.5	94	18.0	77	10.9
	245	99.9	394	100.1	523	100.0	705	99.9

Sources: Wills proved in Prerogative, Consistory, and Archdeaconry Courts in P.R.O. and E.R.O. 1500–1699.

TABLE II: LEADING OCCUPATIONS IN COLCHESTER

1500–79		1580–1619		1620–59		1660–99	
1	Clothier	1	Clothier	1	Baymaker	1	Weaver
2	Mariner	2	Mariner	2	Weaver	2	Baymaker
3	Weaver	3	Weaver	3	Mariner	3	Mariner
4	Smith	4	Baymaker	4	Merchant	4	Shoemaker
5	Tailor	5	Shoemaker	5	Shoemaker	5	Carpenter
6	Butcher	6	Tailor	6	Tailor	6	Woolcomber
7=	Mercer	7=	Draper	7=	Brewer	7	Grocer
	Shearman		Merchant		Draper	8=	Draper
9=	Brewer	9	Baker	9	Miller		Merchant
	Carpenter	10=	Butcher	10=	Baker	10	Tailor
11=	Merchant		Brewer		Clothier	11=	Cardmaker
	Miller	12	Carpenter	12=	Grocer		Maltster
					Innholder		Miller
							Webster

Note: Baymaker includes saymaker; smith includes blacksmith; weaver includes weavers of all types of cloth; draper includes woollendraper and linendraper; mariner includes shipsmaster and sailor.

Sources: Wills proved in Prerogative, Consistory, and Archdeaconry Courts in P.R.O. and E.R.O. 1500–1699.

simply gentlemen and the others a tallow chandler, a brewer, and a yeoman. The lists are dominated by the wealth of John Christmas, assessed initially at £1,000 in movable goods, then at £600, and finally at £400. He was the son of the merchant and bailiff Thomas Christmas, who at his death in 1520 owned lands and houses in St. Runwald's, St. Botolph's, St. Mary's-at-the-Walls, St. Leonard's, St. Martin's, and Holy Trinity parishes, and in Mile End, Greenstead, Lexden, and Old Heath. He also held manors in Bradwell-on-Sea, Beaumont cum Moze, and the unidentified 'Downwell', besides land in Birch,

Copford, Clacton, Kirby-le-Soken, Mundon, Thorpe-le-Soken, and South Han-
ningfield, and Newbridge mill in West Bergholt. He bequeathed 200 marks cash
and 100 marks in plate to his wife Joan and a further 200 marks cash to his
daughters. The recorder Thomas Bonham, the town clerk Thomas Audley, Sir
John Rainsford, and the abbot of St. John's were supervisors of his will. His
bequests to his shearmen, fullers, weavers, and 'ginners' indicate the origins of his
wealth, which testifies to the profits that could be made from cloth production and
trade in Colchester, even in a relatively stagnant economy.[6]

Readjustment and Recovery, 1500–1570

The period has been seen either as one of continuing economic decline for English
provincial towns or as one of readjustment and recovery from the late medieval
depression, and the evidence from Colchester tends to support the latter view.[7]
There, as in many towns, the fortunes of the cloth industry were crucial.
Contemporary comment,[8] government legislation,[9] and case studies of Norwich,
Coventry, and York,[10] all testify to the migration of textile production from town
to countryside in the early 16th century, suggesting that the expanding national
cloth production of those years was based on rural areas rather than towns.
Occupational data from wills indicate that the Colchester industry may have been
in decline: the proportion of the occupied male testators engaged in cloth
production fell from almost 30 per cent in the period 1500–39 to 18 per cent in
the period 1540–79.[11] Furthermore, of the 101 burgesses admitted to the freedom
between 1550 and 1570 for whom an occupation is recorded only 16 were textile
workers.[12]

As early as 1528 the Colchester clothmaker John Boswell the younger reported
difficulty in selling his cloths in Colchester Hall in Blackwell Hall cloth market,
London, but his complaint may have been special pleading to extend his credit
with his wool suppliers.[13] The difficulties of the mid-century slump in the English
cloth industry[14] are evident in Colchester not only in an increasing concern with
poverty and unemployment,[15] but also in the charges of sedition levelled at
malcontented clothworkers in 1566. One of three weavers indicted had declared
'we can get no work nor we have no money... Then will up two or three thousand
in Colchester and about Colchester', while another had complained that 'weavers'
occupation is a dead science nowadays and it will never be better before we make
a rising'.[16]

In 1515 there were arrears of almost £10 on the duke of Norfolk's rent roll of
£25 4s. 5d. in the borough.[17] The town was included among those in need of
're-edification' by the statute of 1540, but that and lists of houses destroyed or in
need of repair in Head ward and among the possessions of St. John's abbey may
indicate long-term decay and may indeed be preludes to a concerted renewal.[18] A

[6] P.R.O., PROB 11/19, ff. 28 sqq.

[7] *Towns in Societies*, ed. P. Abrams and E. A. Wrigley,
159–69; *Urban Hist. Yrbk.* (1978), 60–72; *Econ. H.R.* 2nd
ser. xxxix. 182–4.

[8] *Tudor Econ. Doc.* ed. R. H. Tawney and E. Power, iii.
117–18; *Discourse of Commonweal of Realm of Eng.* ed. M.
Dewar, 76–7, 91.

[9] 25 Hen. VIII, c. 18; 1 Mary Stat. III, c. 7; 2 & 3 Ph.
& Mary, c. 11; 4 & 5 Ph. & Mary, c. 5.

[10] *Towns in Societies*, 178–9; *Past and Present*, xl. 61; W.
R. D. Jones, *Mid-Tudor Crisis 1539–1563*, 122–3; *Past and
Present*, xxxiv. 49–69; C. Phythian-Adams, *Desolation of a
City*, 31–67; D. Palliser, *Tudor York*, 162, 201, 208–10.

[11] Sources cited for Tables I and II.

[12] Burgess admissions extracted from E.R.O., D/B 5 Cr117–
134.   [13] *L. & P. Hen. VIII*, iv (2), p. 1831.

[14] *Econ. H.R.* 1st ser. x. 153, 160; G. D. Ramsay, *Eng.
Overseas Trade During the Centuries of Emergence*, 22; J. D.
Gould, *Great Debasement: Currency and the Economy in
mid-Tudor Eng.* 140–1.

[15] Below, this chapter, Soc. Structure (Early 16th century).

[16] *Cal. Assize Rec. Essex, Eliz. I*, p. 51; F. G. Emmison,
Elizabethan Life: Disorder, 62–4.   [17] B.L. Add. Ch. 215.

[18] 32 Hen. VIII, c. 18; E.R.O., D/Y 2/2, p. 13; P.R.O.,
E 310/13/40; *Urban Hist. Yearbk.* (1978), 63; below, this
chapter, Topography (Town to 1640).

much longer list of the abbey's lands in 1539 gives no suggestion of general decay.[19] The occasional record of decay in the chamberlain's account for 1548–9 is offset by more frequent references to new buildings, and many more townsmen were assessed for subsidy on land and houses in 1547 than in 1524–5.[20] In 1550 the corporation thought it worthwhile to invest £284 5s. in buying former chantry lands and houses in Colchester and the surrounding parishes.[21] Monastic or chantry lands changed hands time and again in later 16th-century Colchester, providing a significant stimulus to the land market, and John Lucas's acquisition of St. John's Abbey provided the townsmen with the custom of a substantial landed seat to replace that lost by the demise of the monastery.[22]

Returns of Colchester's overseas and inland trade in the earlier 16th century were included under those for the headport of Ipswich. If the Ipswich figures reflect Colchester's experience, the later 15th and early 16th centuries witnessed expansion rather than decline, and the town may have escaped the recession that affected so many provincial ports between the 1520s and 1550s as trade became increasingly concentrated upon London.[23] It is also possible that the growth of coastal traffic benefited Colchester as it did other east coast ports in the earlier 16th century; a predominantly coastal trade may explain the small average tonnage of the 23 vessels belonging to the town in 1550.[24] The annual farm of tolls and profits of the Hythe, which may have fallen from £29 in 1501–2 to £24 in 1504–5 and then rose only to £28 in 1521–2, the sum still paid in 1548–9, is not necessarily a reliable index.[25] There were difficulties with the Colne channel, which in 1536 had reportedly been 'much filled' with silt for 10 or 12 years past. A voluntary collection for its repair failed to raise a sufficient sum, and in 1549 a rate was levied on the borough which, with other contributions, yielded £290 for repairs.[26]

Ordinances enacted in the 1560s provide indirect evidence of the level of internal trade. Between 1562 and 1565 the corporation showed considerable concern with the regulation of marketing in general and that of 'foreigners' or non-freemen in particular.[27] Careful licensing of chandlers was introduced to ensure adequate provisions and fair prices. Detailed charges were imposed upon all 'foreigners' buying hides and skins in Colchester market, while every tanner was enjoined to bring as much tanned leather into the market as he took hides and skins out. The two wardens of the butchers continued to be sworn annually, one chosen by the butchers and the other by the bailiffs and aldermen. No 'foreign' butcher was to sell meat in the market after 2 p.m. between All Saints' and Shrove Tuesday, and after 3 p.m. between Easter and All Saints'. Only butchers living in the town and those who had served a seven-year apprenticeship might be admitted free, but a butcher's widow might carry on his trade. Other regulations were designed to ensure adequate quality and supply of meat. New regulations were enacted for the fishery in 1567 when there were said to be twice the customary number of oyster dredgers.[28] Only those licensed by the bailiffs were to dredge for oysters, on pain

[19] P.R.O., SC 6/Hen. VIII/976.
[20] B.L. Stowe MS. 829, ff. 12–40; below, this chapter, Soc. Structure (Early 16th century).
[21] E.R.O., Boro. Mun. Acc. C1: Misc. Deeds, item 2; Cal. Pat. 1549–51, 420–1.
[22] Cal. Pat. 1547–8, 204, 252–7; 1548–9, 86; below, Religious Houses.
[23] D. Burwash, Eng. Merchant Shipping 1460–1540, 145–64 and App. II, Tables of Group IV; E. M. Carus-Wilson and

O. Coleman, Eng.'s Export Trade 1275–1547, 71–4, 114–19; R. Davis, Eng. Overseas Trade 1500–1700, Table 1, 52.
[24] Econ. H.R. 2nd ser. xiii. 338–9.
[25] Britnell, Growth and Decline, 278; Bodl. MS. Rolls Essex 2; B.L. Stowe MS. 829, f. 14.
[26] E.R.O., D/B 5 R2, loose fol.; B.L. Stowe MS. 829, ff. 26 and v., 55 and v.
[27] E.R.O., D/B 5 R5, ff. 91v.–92v., 93v., 102–104v.
[28] Ibid. ff. 111–12.

of 40s. fine, while all oysters, mackerel, and other fish were to be sold in the market at the Hythe, unless bought by householders for their own consumption.

A more general attempt to regulate economic activity was made in 1562, when the town was said to be very much decayed by immigrants intent on 'their own singular lucre', whose activities brought into contempt the authority of the corporation. The main problem was those non-freemen who kept open shops and warehouses in Colchester and thus profited from the town without contributing to it. No 'foreign' retailer or artisan was to live in the borough unless he first compounded with the bailiffs and aldermen for his freedom or for his foreign fine, on pain of 40s. No 'foreigner' was to buy any corn, grain, salt, coal, herring, fish, merchandise, or anything else from any other 'foreigner', on pain of forfeiture. No goods were to be 'foreign bought and sold' without payment of appropriate fines, while inhabitants were required to sue only in the borough courts unless granted special licence to sue elsewhere.[29] Taken together the ordinances represent a concerted attempt by the corporation to keep control over economic activity in the town, to protect the interests of the inhabitants, particularly of the freemen, against a perceived threat from the activities of outsiders. In 1565 regulations for taking up the freedom by birth were tightened.[30]

Had the town still been in economic decline there would have been little need to protect the burgesses from competition, and further proof of the borough's attraction to traders is provided by the limits and bounds of St. Dennis's or the Pardon Fair set out in 1562. On the south side of High Street stood fletchers, bowyers, saddlers, collarmakers, ropers, glovers, smiths, haberdashers, holland-shiremen, grocers, linendrapers, and mercers, their stalls extending from East gate to St. Runwald's church. On the north side of the road were the fishmongers and salters, then the shoemakers whose stalls extended up to the butchers' shambles. 'Foreign' linendrapers were set apart, and next to them were the pewterers, brasiers, and tinkers, town dwellers or 'foreign', followed by the tanners and soapers, who stood near St. Runwald's church. Beyond them, towards the cornmarket, stood nailmen, ironmongers, 'Ipswich men being coverlet men', foreign woollendrapers and hosiers, turners, basketmakers, 'bowlmen', and traders in butter, cheese, and corn. The goldsmiths also had an appropriate, but unspecified, location. The injunction that stalls were only to line the streets and not to be placed crossways or alongside each other implies competition for space, a bustling hive of activity for the eight days of the fair.[31] It may well be that in mid 16th-century Colchester, as in Norwich, increasing internal trade and manufacture for home consumption compensated for a depressed textile industry.[32]

The number of burgesses admitted to the town supports that interpretation. The total admitted each decade by purchase remained roughly stable during the earlier 16th century, at a level comparable to that of the later 15th.[33] That it was still proving difficult to attract migrants is perhaps suggested by the frequent concession of 3s. 4d. of the standard 23s. 4d. fine early in the century, until a sum of 20s. became the norm in the 1530s.[34] Evidence of the desire to attract inhabitants of the right calibre is provided by the agreement to reduce the fine payable by John Neve, clothmaker, of Stowmarket in 1516, from 20s. to 10s. provided he remained in

[29] Ibid. ff. 90v.–91v.
[30] Ibid. ff. 107v.–108; below, this chapter, Boro. Govt.
[31] E.R.O., D/B 5 R5, ff. 89v.–90.
[32] Past and Present, xxxiv. 49–69.

[33] Burgess admissions from E.R.O., D/B 5 Cr83–163; D/B 5 Cb1/2–4; D/B 5 Cb2/2–4. Figures for 15th cent. are in Britnell, Growth and Decline, 279–80.
[34] E.R.O., D/B 5 Cr82–109.

Colchester for at least five years. Remain he did, immediately becoming a common councillor, later an alderman, and eventually bailiff four times before his death in 1542.[35] He was among the wealthiest townsmen in the 1520s, being assessed for subsidy on £40 in goods. By 1542 his wealth had increased substantially, and he left £400 to buy lands and houses worth £20 a year to pay annuities.[36] In the 1550s there was a decisive increase in the numbers purchasing the freedom of the town, to 107 from 59 in the 1540s. If the complaints of the 1560s are to be believed, many more were assuming the freemen's privileges without paying for them. Despite the textile depression a distinct quickening of economic activity is evident in mid 16th-century Colchester, enough to sustain the urban economy through a difficult period for its staple industry and to permit some demographic growth across the second and third quarters of the century.

Growth and Development, 1570–1700

The town's economy grew decisively in the final third of the 16th century, and the key to that growth was the revival of its cloth industry. The lesson of the mid-century crisis in the English cloth export trade was that demand for the traditional heavy woollen product was inelastic, and that it was dangerous to rely so heavily upon one type of cloth,[37] whether exported in its raw state or dyed and dressed as in Colchester. Innovation was widespread, and in Colchester such innovation was inspired by the arrival of Dutch immigrants in the 1560s.[38] Late in 1561 the corporation agreed that the bailiff Benjamin Clere should treat with the Privy Council for the taking in of Dutch refugees, and the first 55 persons in 11 households arrived in 1565.[39] In 1571 there were 185 resident aliens, 431 two years later, and 1,291 by 1586. Only then did the influx slow, a census of 1622 recording 1,535 aliens.[40] The annual average number of baptisms in the Dutch church in the mid 17th century stood at 48,[41] suggesting that the size of the community had stabilized at about 1,500 in a total population of some 10,500–11,000.

The immigrants were granted considerable privileges, most notably control of the Dutch Bay Hall to which all 'new draperies' were taken for inspection and sealing before sale. Despite recurrent disputes with English weavers during the later 16th and early 17th century those privileges were repeatedly upheld.[42] The introduction of the new worsted draperies, particularly bays and says, was the key contribution of the Dutch, for those cloths were relatively light and cheap, and appealed to a wide market in southern as well as northern Europe.[43] The quality control imposed by the Dutch, although limited in 1631 to bays and says, was crucial to the reputation of the Colchester cloth, which was frequently reported to be sold simply upon inspection of its seals. Colchester bays became a byword for quality in the 17th century, and were still known in the early 18th century 'over most of the trading parts of Europe'.[44]

The revival of the Colchester textile industry is evident from the town's

35 Ibid. D/B 5 Cr87, rot. 23; Cr89, rot. 1; Cr96, rot. 1.
36 P.R.O., E 179/108/147; ibid. PROB 11/29, f. 1.
37 Econ. H.R. 2nd ser. xxii. 423–5.
38 Immigrants and Minorities, i. 261–80.
39 E.R.O., D/B 5 R5, f. 92; Roker, 'Flemish and Dutch in Colch.' 85.
40 P.R.O., SP 12/78, no. 9; SP 12/190, no. 2; SP 14/129, no. 70; E.R.O., D/B 5 R7, ff. 296v.–299.
41 Calculated from Reg. Dutch Ch. of Colch. (Huguenot

Soc. xii).
42 Immigrants and Minorities, i. 266, 269–72.
43 Econ. H.R. 2nd ser. xxii. 424; Ramsay, Eng. Overseas Trade, 50–4; Davis, Eng. Overseas Trade, 20–5; Univ. Birmingham Hist. Jnl. vii. 50–1.
44 Cal. S.P. Dom. 1619–23, 247; 1635, 266–7; Acts of P.C. 1592, 76; 1630–1, 200; Hist. MSS. Com. 2, 3rd Rep. p. 71; Hist. MSS. Com. 6, 7th Rep. I, H.L., p. 131; Hist. MSS. Com. 7, 8th Rep. I, H.L., p. 134; D. Defoe, Tour, ed. G. D. H. Cole (1927), i. 17.

occupational structure (Tables I and II). In the period 1580–1619 the percentage of the occupied population engaged in cloth production and distribution rose to 26, with baymaker fourth among the town's leading occupations. By the period 1620–59 baymakers had achieved first position, and 37 per cent of the occupied male population was employed in cloth production and sale. That figure rose to 40 per cent later in the century, by which time Continental producers were attempting to emulate the English product.[45] In the period 1660–99, only 2 clothiers, 3 clothworkers, and 3 dyers were found in a sample of 705 occupations, showing that the dominance of the new draperies over the old in Colchester was complete. Occupations of Colchester apprentices enrolled between 1580 and 1630 tell the same story, the proportion involved in textile production rising from little more than a quarter in the 1580s to almost a half in each of the first three decades of the 17th century.[46] In 1629 it was claimed, with typical exaggeration, that 20,000 persons were maintained by bay and say manufacture in Colchester alone, producing 400 bays and as many says each week.[47] In the early 18th century it was suggested that the town returned '£30,000 weekly in ready money for these stuffs'.[48] Celia Fiennes found that 'the whole town is employed in spinning, weaving, washing, drying, and dressing their bays',[49] while Defoe's impression was that 'The town may be said chiefly to subsist by the trade of making bays' and that the whole county was employed, and in part maintained, by spinning wool for the bay trade of Colchester and neighbouring towns.[50]

The industry's progress was not entirely trouble free, particularly in the unstable trading conditions of the 1620s and 1630s.[51] Hostility between England and Spain in the 1620s resulted in the prohibition of exports to that important market, reportedly reducing weekly production of Colchester bays from 400 pieces to 50, and leaving over £6,000 worth unsold in 1629, besides says to a similar value.[52] By 1631 Colchester's poor were petitioning against an abatement of their accustomed wages,[53] and in 1635 the bailiffs and J.P.s, in response to another complaint by the bayweavers, imposed a sliding scale of payment, 10s.–12s. a bay depending on the current market value of each ell of cloth.[54] Two years later weavers accused a baymaker of paying low wages and forcing them to accept payment in kind,[55] and attempts to cut costs may have led to the abuses in bay manufacture of which London merchants complained in 1635, a year in which exports from Colchester slumped.[56]

Notwithstanding such vicissitudes, the long-term trend in production of new draperies in Colchester was decidedly upward. The officers of the Dutch Bay Hall collected 'rawboots', fines for faulty workmanship by English manufacturers, which from 1636 provide an index of bay production (Table III). The decennial average figure rose steadily until the 1690s when a combination of poor harvests and warfare caused difficulties for English foreign trade in general.[57] The impact of the siege of Colchester of 1648 is clear, as is that of the plague of 1665–6,[58] but the speed

45 E. Kerridge, *Textile Manufactures in Early Modern Eng.* 242.

46 Apprenticeships from E.R.O., D/B 5 Cr142–186; D/B 5 Cb1/2–9; D/B 5 Cb2/3–11; D/B 5 Gb1–3; Goose, 'Econ. and Social Aspects', Table 3.1, p. 94.

47 *17th Cent. Econ. Doc.* ed. J. Thirsk and J. P. Cooper, 224.

48 T. Cox, *Magna Britannia*, i. 707.

49 *Journeys of Celia Fiennes*, ed. C. Morris, 142.

50 Defoe, *Tour*, i. 17.

51 B. Supple, *Commercial Crisis and Change in Eng. 1600–1642*, 52–8, 108–12, 122–4; *Econ. H.R.* 2nd ser. xxii.

239–40; cf. *Univ. Birmingham Hist. Jnl.* vii. 49.

52 *17th Cent. Doc.* 225.

53 *Acts of P.C.* 1630–1, 358–9; *Cal. S.P. Dom.* 1625–49, 430.

54 E.R.O., D/B 5 Cb1/10, f. 84v.

55 P.R.O., PC 2/47, pp. 389–90; *Cal. S.P. Dom.* 1637, 32, 44, 70, 87–9, 115.

56 P.R.O., PC 2/45, pp. 15, 37–8, 312, 435–6; *Cal. S.P. Dom.* 1635, 266–7, 306, 603; *Econ. H.R.* 2nd ser. xxii. 245.

57 Morant, *Colch.* 79; D. C. Coleman, *Econ. of Eng. 1450–1750*, 135.

58 Above, this chapter, Intro.

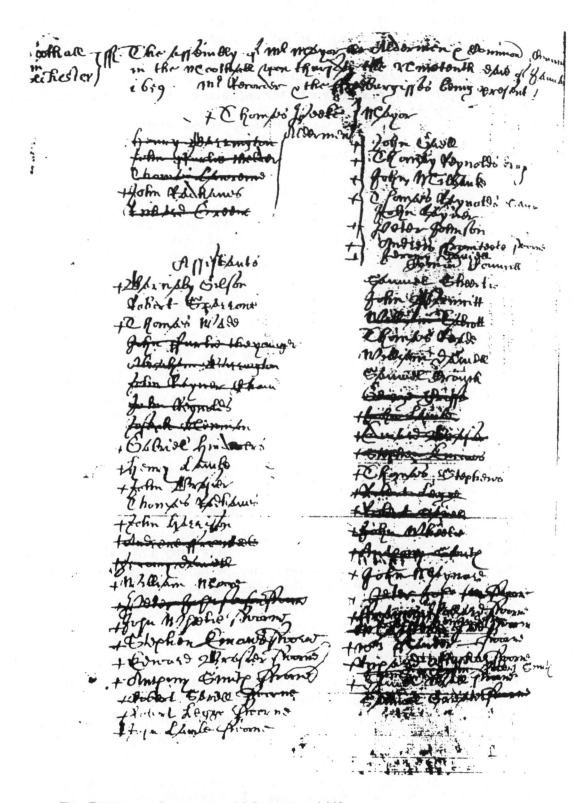

THE BOROUGH ASSEMBLY, 19 JANUARY 1660

list of officers, with the names of those removed from office crossed through; the meeting is dated 19 January 1659 which was 19 January 1660 in the modern calendar

with which production recovered from each setback and then rose to new heights testifies to the resilience of the industry.

Colchester's economy flourished in other ways from the later 16th century. The thrice-weekly market continued to sell a variety of foodstuffs including 'garden stuff', the Dutch having stimulated the development of horticulture.[59] As a corn market Colchester was unrivalled in the county,[60] and the importance of its grain trade in the 17th century is shown by the appearance of maltsters among its leading

TABLE III: 'RAWBOOTS' FINES FOR ENGLISH BAYS

Year	£	Year	£	Year	£	Year	£
1636	33	1652	38	1668	101	1684	233
1637	34	1653	41	1669	115	1685	172
1638	39	1654	61	1670	121	1686	198
1639	39	1655	59	1671	125	1687	200
1640	48	1656	58	1672	120	1688	214
1641	41	1657	55	1673	140	1689	215
1642	25	1658	54	1674	143	1690	188
1643	34	1659	53	1675	139	1691	174
1644	46	1660	83	1676	125	1692	144
1645	53	1661	86	1677	134	1693	128
1646	42	1662	77	1678	139	1694	197
1647	38	1663	94	1679	124	1695	200
1648	36	1664	97	1680	165	1696	183
1649	67	1665	92	1681	188	1697	162
1650	73	1666	31	1682	225	1698	173
1651	49	1667	61	1683	248	1699	174

Source: E.R.O., D/B 5 Gb3–6, *passim*.

tradesmen. Pontage was levied in 1635 on corn, timber, firewood, straw, hay, clay, sand, bricks, tiles, household implements, and wool carried to and from the town by road.[61] Hides, skins, and pelts were particularly important in the town, which possessd its own leather hall.[62] In the later 16th century a new shambles and a new market cross were built, to improve and perhaps enlarge the market.[63] The twice-weekly woolmarket was reorganized in 1592 and 1595 and continued throughout the 17th century. Nevertheless, wool was still sold in inns and private houses, the lessee of the market claiming in 1685 that the aldermen and common councillors were the greatest offenders.[64] In 1624 the meat market was 'of late years much increased', while a succession of complaints against trade in meat and hides after the appointed market hours and outside the market place suggest that private marketing was growing too.[65] The 1693 charter granted a new Tuesday market and a new fair in July; both concentrated on livestock, building upon a long established trade in horses and cattle.[66] Growing numbers of inns, alehouses, and

[59] E.R.O., D/B 5 Gb1, 31 July, 29 Nov. 1592; 6 Nov. 1598; D/B 5 Gb3, ff. 4, 38v.–39, 42v.; Gb4, ff. 217, 227; Gb5, f. 264; J. Norden, *Description of Essex*, 14; Cox, *Magna Britannia*, i. 707; W. Cunningham, *Alien Immigrants to Eng.* 177; E. Kerridge, *Agric. Revolution*, 269; Morant, *Colch.* 76; *Agrarian Hist. Eng. and Wales*, v. 503–7.

[60] F. Hull, 'Agriculture and Rural Society in Essex 1560–1640' (Lond. Univ. Ph.D. thesis, 1950), 127–8.

[61] E.R.O., D/B 5 Gb3, f. 140.

[62] E.R.O., D/B 5 R5, f. 92v.; D/B 5 Gb1, 2 Nov. 1579; Gb2, f. 130v.; D/B 5 Aa1/2, 5, 14; D/Y 2/10, f. 128.

[63] Ibid. D/B 5 Gb1, 2 June 1595; below, Markets.

[64] Ibid. D/B 5 Gb1, 2 June 1595; Gb2, ff. 147v., 185 and v.; Gb4, ff. 54v., 228v.; Gb5, f. 177v.–178v., 238–241v.; Gb6, p. 113.

[65] Ibid. D/B 5 Gb1, 2 Nov. 1579; 6 Nov. 1598; Gb3, ff. 38v.–39; Gb4, f. 150; Gb5, ff. 236, 283v.

[66] P.R.O., PC 2/75, pp. 120–1; PC 2/77, pp. 376–7; *Colch. Charters*, 174; W. Walker, *Essex Markets and Fairs*, 32.

taverns catered for those attending the markets.[67] The increased overland traffic, transporting cloth to and raw wool from London, was probably chiefly responsible for the worsening roads; in 1616 the highways between Colchester (and other Essex towns) and London were being badly damaged by overloaded wagons.[68] By the later 17th century considerable quantities of raw wool were also brought from inland counties, even though the coastal supplies were becoming increasingly important.[69]

The town's overseas trade tended to follow the fortunes of its cloth industry. Port books suggest an expanding export trade in the late 16th century and the early 17th, based chiefly upon the new draperies.[70] Exports of new draperies increased approximately fourfold in the 17th century, with rapid expansions in the periods 1600–30 and 1670–1700, a slump in the 1630s, and a slow recovery to 1670. Exports of traditional woollen cloths, depressed in the 1590s, mirrored the general recovery of that trade in the early 17th century, only to fall off steadily after 1622.[71]

In 1571–2, apart from cloth, Colchester exported hides, leather and leather goods, coal, beer, wax, rough horns, and 'woadnets' (perhaps 'woadnuts' or balls of woad), all in small quantities.[72] In 1607–8 and 1621–2 cloth was supplemented by coal, beer, salt, aquavitae, sheepskins, iron, wax, mustard seed, peas, hats, deal, stockings, cordage, and old wool-cards, while in 1638–9 exports included hops, starch, ginger, cinnamon, paper, lead, copperas, oil, lime, and haberdashery wares.[73] In the later 17th century the range of commodities narrowed while the quantities of particular items increased. A little coal, some old wool-cards, hops, rapeseed, saffron, peas, some clothing, a ton of 'old iron', and the occasional horse appear, but quantities of dressed calfskins, leather, rye, wheat, and oysters dominated the non-textile export trade. Export of oysters grew remarkably, the annual average for the four years 1679–80 and 1700–1 amounting to 1,140 bu., while in the peak year of 1682 over 4,000 bu. were shipped overseas.[74]

Imports also grew and diversified. In 1571–2, apart from various types of cloth, Colchester imported some Spanish wool and unspun cotton, handles for cards and wire, new wool-cards and combs, teazles, and red and green dyestuffs. Several shipments of salt were received, besides luxuries such as sugar, prunes, raisins, pepper, cloves, and ginger. Household items included French knives and drinking glasses, bottles, brown and white paper, pins, and thread.[75] By 1660–1 a great deal of French and Rhenish wine was imported, as was iron, iron wire, iron vessels, oil, and various household items. Battery, copper wire, stone bottles, cordage, quern stones, rope, fish oil, vinegar, spirits, French salt, Spanish salt, Norway deal, 'timber to make cardboard', Holland cheese, clapboards, prunes, cloves, refined sugar, pickled herrings, wine lees, Osnabruck and broad Hamburg cloth and other manufactured items, foodstuffs, and raw materials came to the town, largely from Rotterdam but also from ports in France and Norway.[76] By 1678–80 Dutch and German cloth was becoming more prominent, until between 1699 and 1701 various types of Dutch and German linen (particularly osnaburgs, duck, holland, and burlaps) and broad and narrow German cloths predominated; there were also

[67] P.R.O., SP 12/116, no. 12; *Cal. Pat.* 1569–72, 14–15; E.R.O., D/B 5 Gb2, ff. 119v.–121v.; below, this chapter, Soc. Structure (Economic and Social Regulation).

[68] *Cal. Assize Rec. Essex, Eliz. I*, p. 167.

[69] *C.J.* xiii. 570, 720; K. H. Burley, 'Econ. Development of Essex in later 17th and early 18th cents.' (Lond. Univ. Ph.D. thesis, 1957), 300–2, 310–11; P. J. Bowden, *Wool Trade in Tudor and Stuart Eng.* 66–7; R. B. Westerfield, *Middlemen in Eng. Business*, 262, 269.

[70] *Econ. H.R.* 2nd ser. xxxix. 170–1 and Table 1.

[71] Ibid.; ibid. xxii. 245; P.R.O., E 190/610/3; E 190/610/11; E 190/612/12; E 190/620/4.

[72] P.R.O., E 190/589/7; *O.E.D.* s.v. woad.

[73] P.R.O., E 190/599/5; E 190/602/1; E 190/605/1.

[74] Ibid. E 190/610/3; E 190/610/11; E 190/612/12; E 190/620/4; Burley, 'Econ. Development', 87.

[75] P.R.O., E 190/589/7.

[76] Ibid. E 190/606/5.

ELIZABETH I, FROM HER CHARTER, 1559

CHARLES I, FROM HIS CHARTER, 1635

pantiles and stone of various kinds, stone pots and earthenware, Norway wood, haberdasheries, paper, bullrushes, 'prepared metal', and household goods.[77] By then the range of imports was even wider, still mainly from Rotterdam, indicating the growing importance of Colchester as a centre of consumption and redistribution.

Despite its expanding trade, Colchester was not in the front rank of English provincial ports. Figures for customs payments in the 1590s place it 14th out of the 19 ports for which evidence survives,[78] while on the basis of the annual average cloth custom and subsidy paid by 15 ports between 1600 and 1640 Colchester stood in 10th place, paying less than half the total collected at Ipswich and less than an 11th of that paid by Hull.[79] Most of the growing export trade in the town's new draperies was conducted through London. In 1635, during a dispute with Colchester merchants, the Merchant Adventurers Company claimed that the town could boast only four or five merchants trading overseas, and that those bought only a fraction of the cloth made at Colchester, most bays being taken to London to be bought by the Merchant Adventurers and others.[80] Little had changed by the end of the century. In the four years 1697–1701 the annual average national export of double bays was 36,872 cloths, of which 1,137 (3.1 per cent) were exported directly from Colchester. Only 3.6 per cent of the says, serges, and perpetuanas exported nationally left from Colchester, 0.4 per cent of the single bays, and none of the treble bays.[81] Coastal shipments of bays to London in 1698–9 amounted to nearly 25,000 cloths, twenty times the town's direct exports.[82]

The geographical horizons of Colchester's trade were not extended by its expanding new drapery exports. In 1571–2 Colchester traded almost exclusively with Rouen and la Rochelle in France, with Flushing in the Netherlands, and with 'Camphere' (perhaps Quimper, France, or Kampen, Netherlands). One or two ships went to Bordeaux and Dieppe (France), to Danzig (now Gdansk, Poland), to Hamburg and Stade in Germany, and to the unidentified 'Newhaven'. Imports were additionally received from the unidentified 'Olderne' and 'Borwage' (possibly for Norway), and from Emden (Germany).[83] By the 1590s trade was heavily concentrated upon Middelburg (Netherlands), and in the earlier 17th century on 'Camphere' and Rotterdam. Occasional shipments were made to Seville (Spain), the Spanish Islands and the Azores, but the bay trade to the Mediterranean was dominated by London.[84] Colchester played little part in the Eastland trade in which Ipswich was so heavily involved.[85] Only an occasional Colchester vessel sailed to the Baltic between the 1560s and 1590s, and relatively few thereafter apart from flurries of activity in the 1600s, the 1680s, and at the very end of the 17th century, which never exceeded seven passages each way in any one year.[86] The alderman John Hunwick was a member of the Eastland Co. and of the Spanish and Portuguese Cos. in 1583. His apprentice John Eldred was a member of the Eastland

77 Ibid. E 190/610/3; E 190/610/11; E 190/619/12; E 190/620/4.

78 Calculated from Hist. MSS. Com. 9, Salisbury, v. 393; T. S. Willan, Studies in Elizabethan Foreign Trade, 75.

79 Calculated from Econ. H.R. 2nd ser. xxii. 244–6.

80 Cal. S.P. Dom. 1635, 103.

81 P.R.O., E 190/612/12; E 190/620/4; Burley, 'Econ. Development', Table XL; calculated from E. B. Schumpeter, Eng. Overseas Trade Statistics 1697–1808, Table XIV, and p. 44.

82 P.R.O., E 190/618/15; E 190/618/18.

83 Ibid. E 190/589/7.

84 Ibid. E 190/599/6; E 190/602/1; E 190/605/1; Cal. S.P. Dom. 1625–49, 121; 1629–31, 209; 1631–3, 27; Willan, Studies in Foreign Trade, 75; A. Friis, Alderman Cockayne's Project and the Cloth Trade, 65, 116, 128.

85 R. W. K. Hinton, Eastland Trade and the Commonweal in 17th Cent.; J. Fedorowicz, Eng.'s Baltic Trade in Early 17th Cent.: Study of Anglo-Polish Diplomacy; H. Zins, Eng. and Baltic in Elizabethan Era.

86 N. E. Bang, Tabeller over Skibsfart og Varetransport gennem Oresund 1497–1660; N. E. Bang and K. Korst, Tabeller over Skibsfart og Varetransport gennem Oresund 1661–1783.

Co. by 1608, and of the Muscovy Co. by 1624.[87] John Braxted was described as a merchant adventurer in 1604,[88] and although in 1619 the town claimed to have no merchants free of any company John Wiles of Colchester, who had served his apprenticeship with John Eldred, was a merchant adventurer in 1622.[89] In 1634, however, the restoration of the privileges of the Merchant Adventurers Co. of London led to a Privy Council order confining Colchester merchants to trade with Rotterdam.[90] Despite occasional shipments to Norway, Hamburg (Germany), Dunkirk and Bordeaux in France, and 'Stockholland', the Rotterdam connexion dominated the town's overseas trade throughout the later 17th century and into the 18th.[91]

Colchester's coastal trade centred upon London throughout the later 16th and 17th centuries. In 1568–9 cheese and butter were the main goods sent to the capital, followed by wheat, oats, malt, wood, and faggots. A greater variety of products was received in return, notably dyestuffs, soap, oil, groceries, ironware, coal, and canvas. A few shipments of butter and cheese went to Faversham, Gravesend, and Sittingbourne (Kent), occasional journeys were made to Southampton and Exeter, while Newcastle received considerable quantities of rye. Trade with Newcastle was second in importance only to that with London: of 77 inward cargoes in 1568–9, 44 were from London and 25 from Newcastle, the latter consisting largely of coal and salt.[92] Colchester merchants had been sending grain to Newcastle since the early 16th century, when Ambrose Lowth was accused of attempting to store a shipment of wheat and rye at Newcastle until he could set his own price.[93] In 1510 Lowth was presented in the borough court for regrating salt coming to Colchester market.[94] By the 1590s, Colchester vessels were venturing to the Scottish coast for salt.[95]

The importance of the coastal connexion with London grew as bay and say manufacture developed, until by 1649 two vessels laden with draperies sailed twice a week between Colchester and London.[96] Towards the end of the century the exchange of cloth for wool dominated the traffic, and by 1698–9 as many as 117 of 135 outward coastal cargoes were destined for London. London-bound cargoes contained coarse locks, grain, potash, household goods, ironware, beeswax, groceries and spices, leather, and foreign linens, many presumably imported from Rotterdam. Large quantities of wool for textile manufacture were received in return, followed in importance by oil, soap, tobacco, wine, iron, and various drapery, grocery, and household wares. Ten cargoes to Newcastle, four to Sunderland, and three to Whitby, consisted largely of rye and peas, supplemented by barley, beans, hay, chairs, and 'many other goods', whose diversity apparently defeated the patience of the customs officers.[97]

In 1619 Colchester possessed 26 vessels, including fishing boats and hoys, the six largest being coal ships averaging c. 100 tons.[98] By 1702–4 the 25 Colchester vessels involved in the coal trade with Newcastle averaged c. 48 tons.[99] In 1612, out of a total of 2,407 shipments of coal from Newcastle, 48 were made in Colchester ships, placing the town tenth among provincial ports involved in the trade, while a return of the tax collected under the new coal excise in 1651 places Colchester eighth of 57 provincial ports.[1] By the end of the

[87] E.R.O., D/B 5 Cr145, rot. 8d.; D/B 5 Cb2/7, f. 191; *Acts of P.C.* 1623–5, 393. [88] E.R.O., D/B 5 Cb1/5, f. 416v.

[89] P.R.O., SP 14/105, no. 114; E.R.O., D/B 5 Cb2/7, f. 191; Friis, *Alderman Cockayne*, 116.

[90] P.R.O., PC 2/45, p. 15.

[91] Ibid. E 190/606/5; E 190/610/3; E 190/610/11; E 190/619/12; E 190/620/4; E 190/627/8; *Bull. Inst. Hist. Res.* xxix. 229–30.

[92] P.R.O., E 190/587/10; E 190/588/1; Hist. MSS. Com. 73, *Exeter*, 375. [93] P.R.O., REQ 2/12, no. 206.

[94] E.R.O., D/B 5 Cr83, rot. 1d.

[95] Hist. MSS. Com. 9, *Salisbury*, iv. 543–4.

[96] *Cal. S.P. Dom.* 1649–50, 317.

[97] P.R.O., E 190/618/15; E 190/618/18.

[98] Ibid. SP 14/105, no. 114.

[99] Westerfield, *Middlemen*, 229 n.

[1] P.R.O., SP 18/17, no. 93; J. U. Nef, *Rise of Brit. Coal Ind.* ii. 26 n. London and Newcastle are excluded from the calculations.

17th century Sunderland had overhauled Newcastle as the main source of coal. In 1698–9 as many as 47 cargoes of coal were received from Sunderland, only 27 from Newcastle, but the latter also contained salt, glass, tanned calfskins, butter, and grindstones. Other imports, mainly of raw wool and fuller's earth, came largely from Kentish ports, particularly Rochester and Faversham.[2]

Colchester's developing trade led to a fairly steady growth in the mercantile tonnage owned by the town (Table IV). The check in that growth in the late 16th and early 17th centuries may well have been due to the increased involvement in Colchester trade of merchants from the Low Countries. Whereas in 1571–2 London merchants had competed for Colchester cloth exports, in the exceptional year 1605 'strangers' carried 1,095 double and 614 single bays out of the town.[3] In 1621–2 while trade with Rotterdam, Calais, and

TABLE IV: COLCHESTER SHIPPING

Date	Number of Vessels	Total Tonnage
1550	23	840
1582	42	1,246
1619	26	c. 1,080
1629	13	1,460
1676	49	c. 3,930
1702	34	3,675

Sources: 1550, G. V. Scammell, 'English Merchant Shipping at the end of the Middle Ages: some East Coast Evidence', *Econ. H.R.* 2nd ser. xiii. 338; 1582, P.R.O., SP 12/156/45; 1619, P.R.O., SP 14/105/114; 1629, 1676, 1702, Burley, 'Econ. Development', Table XIII.

the Azores was dominated by Colchester and Wivenhoe vessels, shipments to 'Camphere', 'Rickade' and 'Crill', c. 40 per cent of exports, were monopolized by 'strangers'.[4] There may have been some truth in the town's complaint in 1616 that a 'great concourse of strangers' shipped into the port and carried away the goods of both English and Dutch merchants, and in the claims made in 1616 and 1619 that Colchester's shipping was much decayed.[5] Shipping had recovered by 1629, and the middle years of the century saw considerable growth. By the end of the century Colchester vessels and Colchester merchants dominated the town's export trade, importing Dutch and German linens and a vast array of other products from Rotterdam, and also wood, iron, and pitch from Norway.[6] In 1582 there were 106 mariners in the town, 344 by 1702.[7] The annual rent payable for the lease of the tolls and profits of the Hythe increased only from £24 in 1504–5 to £42–£44 between 1597 and 1665, but whereas no fine appears to have been paid for the lease in 1504–5, and only 30s. in 1597, the sum charged in 1642 was £101 and in 1665 £150.[8] Through a combination of its overseas and coastal trade Colchester had done far more than hold its own in the face of the increasing activities of the capital, and it was described in 1707 as very rich and populous, inhabited by merchants of considerable estates and great traders.[9]

[2] P.R.O., E 190/618/15; E 190/618/18; T. S. Willan, *Eng. Coasting Trade 1600–1750*, 120–1, 124, 130, 137, 139, 141; C. W. Chalklin, *17th-Cent. Kent*, 177–8.
[3] P.R.O., E 190/589/7; ibid. SP 14/17, no. 66.
[4] Ibid. E 190/602/1.
[5] *Cal. S.P. Dom.* 1616–17, 59–60; P.R.O., SP 14/105, no. 114.
[6] P.R.O., E 190/606/5; E 190/610/3; E 190/610/11;
E 190/619/12; E190/620/4.
[7] P.R.O., SP 12/156, no. 45; Burley, 'Econ. Development', 240.
[8] E.R.O., D/B 5 R2, f. 78v.; D/B 5 Gb1, 3 Aug. 1597; Gb3, f. 229v.; Gb4, f. 314.
[9] J. Brome, *Travels Over Eng., Scotland and Wales*, 112.

SOCIAL STRUCTURE

BETWEEN the 1520s and the 1670s Colchester's population perhaps trebled and its relative size in comparison with other provincial towns increased slightly, from seventh in terms of taxable population in 1524–5 to sixth in terms of recorded hearths in the 1670s.[10] Economic growth undoubtedly accompanied demographic

TABLE V: DISTRIBUTION OF TAXABLE WEALTH 1523–5

	No. of Taxpayers	per cent	Taxable Wealth (to nearest £)	per cent
Wages:				
at £1	402	40.4	402	6.1
over £1	82	8.2	160	2.4
Goods or Lands:				
£2–4	305	30.6	763	11.5
£5–9	77	7.7	502	7.6
£10–19	69	6.9	889	13.4
£20–39	27	2.7	658	9.9
£40–99	25	2.5	1,218	18.4
£100 or more	9	0.9	2,028	30.6
	996	99.9	6,620	99.9

Note: The returns for the 3 years 1523–5 have been conflated by nominative linkage because it is clear that the assessments of the wealthiest individuals were substantially scaled down in 1524 and 1525, and because the substantial differences between the lists for 1524 and 1525 can be explained partly by tax evasion, perhaps particularly among wage-earners. For fuller discussion of this methodology, see Goose, 'Econ. and Social Aspects', 57–62.

Sources: P.R.O., E 179/108/147; E 179/108/162; E 179/108/169.

growth, the town successfully overcoming periods of difficulty, short-lived reversals and slumps, and the impact of plague and the Civil War, but the price which it paid for its success was a greater polarization of society between rich and poor.

Social Structure in the Early 16th Century

Already in the mid 1520s Colchester, like other English towns, exhibited a steeply graduated hierarchy of wealth (Table V).[11] Of the 996 taxpayers recorded in Colchester between 1523 and 1525, 484 (49 per cent) were assessed on wages,[12] a figure comparable with those for other towns whether or not they were centres of cloth production.[13] Other wage earners may have been assessed on goods and yet others may have evaded taxation in both 1524 and 1525 as many apparently did in each year (Table VI). Dependent wage earners thus probably made up at least half the adult male population in the 1520s.

[10] Goose, 'Econ. and Social Aspects', p. 37.
[11] e.g. J. Pound, *Tudor and Stuart Norwich*, 31–3; D. Palliser, *Tudor York*, 134–8; W. T. MacCaffrey, *Exeter 1540–1640*, 247–50; *V.C.H. Oxon.* iv. 101–3; *V.C.H. Glos.* iv. 81.
[12] P.R.O., E 179/108/147, 162, 169. The more comprehensive 1525 list alone produces a slightly lower ratio of 43 per cent.

[13] C. Platt, *Med. Southampton*, 264 sqq.; Hoskins, *Provincial Eng.* 83–4; MacAffrey, *Exeter*, 12, 250; *V.C.H. Yorks. E.R.* i. 159; A. D. Dyer, *City of Worcester in 16th Cent.* 175; *V.C.H. Oxon.* iv. 102; *Northants. Past and Present*, vi. Table 1; Palliser, *Tudor York*, 136–7; *Early Modern Town*, ed. P. Clark, 130–1.

Only eight people were assessed on lands or houses, and all of them except for Thomas Audley's mother-in-law Elizabeth Barnardiston, assessed in 1524 on £55 worth, held estates worth less than £10. That such a high proportion of taxpayers paid on their movables presumably reflects the depths to which land values had

TABLE VI: COMPOSITION OF CONFLATED LISTS OF TAXPAYERS 1524-5

	All Taxpayers	Wages Only
Number in 1524 list	758	356
Number in 1525 list	783	333
Number in both lists	545	150
Number in 1524 list only	213	161
Number in 1525 list only	238	173
Total number of taxpayers	996	484

Sources: P.R.O., E 179/108/162; E 179/108/169.

sunk by the early 16th century.[14] In 1547, by contrast, 50 out of 286 people (17 per cent) paid on lands,[15] a figure which may suggest the growing attractiveness of investment in urban property. In 1628, after a century of population growth and inflation, 125 of 261 taxpayers (48 per cent) were assessed on land or houses rather than on movable goods or as aliens.[16]

Nine people were taxed on £100 or more (Table V), fewer than in Norwich or Exeter, much the same as in Kings Lynn and Bury St. Edmunds, more than in Great Yarmouth, Worcester, York, or Southampton.[17] Those nine, less than 1 per cent of the taxable population, owned as much as 30 per cent of the taxable wealth in the town. The 34 individuals, only 3.4 per cent of the taxable population, who were recognized as rich and required to pay in anticipation on goods worth £40 or more, owned virtually half the town's taxable wealth.

As in other towns, c. 80 per cent of the taxable population paid on £4 or less in goods or wages.[18] They were not all 'poor', as real wages were remarkably high in the early 16th century; in both Coventry and Cambridge substantial numbers assessed in the £2-£4 range kept servants.[19] The occupations of 83 men assessed on goods worth £2-£4 have been identified; they followed 34 different trades, and included 8 weavers, 5 shoemakers, 5 carpenters, 5 mariners, 4 husbandmen, 4 tailors, 4 tanners, 4 barbers, and 4 labourers. Occupations could be traced for 66 wage earners, in 33 trades, including 6 shoemakers or cordwainers, 5 mariners or watermen, 4 weavers, 4 cappers, and 4 butchers. A few people were truly indigent: in 1510 William Baker was accused of harbouring beggars and in 1514 a tailor was indicted for keeping and lodging beggars and vagabonds,[20] but both poverty and vagrancy were lesser problems than they were to become in the early 17th century.

---

[14] Hoskins, *Provincial Eng.* 77-8; *Northern Hist.* xiv. 72-3; *Southern Hist.* i. 42-3. [15] P.R.O., E 179/109/308.

[16] Ibid. E 179/112/643.

[17] Pound, *Norwich*, 33; MacCaffrey, *Exeter*, 248; Dyer, *Worcester*, 175; Palliser, *Tudor York*, 136-7.

[18] Dyer, *Worcester*, 175; *Northants. Past and Present*, vi. 74; *V.C.H. Oxon.* iv. 102; MacCaffrey, *Exeter*, 250; *Early Modern Town*, ed. Clark, 131; *V.C.H. Yorks. E.R.* i. 159;

Goose, 'Econ. and Social Aspects', 75.

[19] Phythian-Adams, *Desolation of a City*, 133-4; *Economica*, xxiii. 296-314; J. Hatcher, *Plague, Population and the Eng. Econ. 1348--1530*, 50; F. R. H. du Boulay, *Age of Ambition*, 13-16, 35-41. In Cambridge 28 (41 per cent) of those identified as employing servants fell into the £2-£4 assessment band: Goose, 'Econ. and Social Aspects', 73-4.

[20] E.R.O., D/B 5 Cr82, rot. 10; D/B 5 Cr86, rot. 5.

The Growth of Poverty, and Poor Relief

The price of wheat in Colchester rose from 5*s.* a quarter in August 1510 to 6*s.* 6*d.* in November that year, to 8*s.* in December 1511, and to between 12*s.* and 13*s.* 6*d.* in the winter 1512–13, before falling to 8*s.* a quarter in October 1514 and to 6*s.* in November.[21] By 1560 wheat prices had approximately doubled, to 24*s.* a quarter, but fell to 20*s.* a quarter in 1566 and 16*s.* a quarter in 1567.[22] In 1577 wheat was 22*s.* 6*d.* a quarter.[23] Long-term inflation and short-term fluctuations in the price of grain, and hence of bread, severely affected the urban poor. It is little wonder that in 1570 the bailiffs complained to the Privy Council that the common estate of the town had decayed.[24]

In 1557, a year of both dearth and sickness, the corporation introduced a compulsory poor rate of 8*d.* in the noble on all houses worth more than 3*s.* 4*d.* a year, to be assessed by specially appointed parish officers. Householders were forbidden to receive any stranger unless he could show that he would not fall to begging. Those accepting 'gatherers and collectors of wood' as tenants, or buying their wood, were to be fined.[25] In 1562 the corporation ordered that alms be collected at every sermon for the relief of the poor and impotent.[26] The alms were regularly collected between 1579 and 1595, as much as 52*s.* 6*d.* being given in 1588–9.[27]

The loss of St. Mary Magdalen's hospital and of other, poorly endowed, medieval hospitals and almshouses may have exacerbated the problem of the poor, although in 1563 the borough was using St. Catherine's hospital as a workhouse. In 1565 the corporation ordered the establishment of a common hospital for 'idle youths and poor children' born in the town, to be financed by the inclosure and letting of some of the half-year lands.[28] The hospital was being built in the early 1570s,[29] children from the poorhouse were baptized at St. Mary's-at-the-Walls in 1574, and in 1579 Richard Hall, proctor of the Colchester poorhouse, was granted protection to gather contributions in Essex and Hertfordshire.[30]

In 1572, in 12 of the town's 16 parishes,[31] 300 people paid poor rate; 102 people, almost all apparently heads of households, received relief. As the population of those parishes was *c.* 3,700,[32] it seems that *c.* 8 per cent of the total population paid a poor rate which was distributed to just under 3 per cent, excluding dependents. Assuming an average household of 4.5 people, and 2.2 in pauper households,[33] over 36 per cent of households contributed, while over 12 per cent (*c.* 224 people or 6 per cent of the total population) received relief. Of 102 named recipients, 44 were widows. Four orphans were being maintained by St. Leonard's parish, and two men in St. Mary Magdalen's were burdened 'with a charge of children'.[34]

In 1582, in the whole town, 114 people received weekly payments, a slightly lower proportion of the total population than ten years earlier. The number of

[21] Ibid. D/B 5 Cr82, rot. 29; Cr83, rot. 6; Cr85, rott. 14, 15; Cr86, rot. 30.

[22] E.R.O., D/B 5 R5, ff. 87v., 94, 95, 96 and v., 100 and v., 106, 109v.   [23] Ibid. D/B 5 Cr140, rot. 2d.

[24] E. L. Cutts, *Colch.* 154–5.

[25] E.R.O., D/Y 2/2, pp. 37–8.   [26] Ibid. D/B 5 R5, f. 94v.

[27] Ibid. D/Y 2/2, pp. 42–59; ibid. Boro. Mun., Acc. C1, Contribution Book to the Poor, unfoliated, end of vol.

[28] *Cal. Pat.* 1547–8, 356; 1557–8, 249; 1560–3, 415; 1563–6, 237; E.R.O., D/B 5 R5, ff. 106v.–107.

[29] E.R.O., D/ACR 6/219; P.R.O., PROB 11/54, f. 17;

PROB 11/55, f. 2.

[30] E.R.O., D/P 246/1/1; Hist. MSS. Com. 9, *Salisbury*, xiii. 170.

[31] E.R.O., D/B 5 R7, ff. 307–18.

[32] Estimate based upon extant parish registers for 6 parishes, adjusted in proportion to numbers given in 1534 return of those swearing fealty to the king.

[33] *Population Studies*, xxiii. 199–224; *Social Hist.* v. 363–4; *Crisis and Order in Eng. Towns 1500–1700*, ed. P. Clark and P. Slack, 177.

[34] E.R.O., D/B 5 R7, ff. 307v., 309v., 311v.

paupers varied widely from parish to parish. None was known in St. Runwald's or St. Martin's, but 20 weekly payments were made in St. Giles's, many of them to widows and other women and several for keeping children. A total of 513 people made regular contributions to the poor rate, suggesting some expansion of the tax base since 1572, the sum collected weekly amounting to 52s. 9¾d.[35]

An array of fines was also devoted to poor relief, including those for overstocking the commons, for breaching the statute of artificers or the assize of bread and of ale, for inadequate tanning of leather, for refusing office, and for not wearing livery gowns to meetings of the borough assembly.[36] The 'rawboots' fines (Table III) were distributed to the poor from 1586 or earlier,[37] as were proceeds from the town lottery and rents from some town land, probably inclosed half-year land.[38] In 1652 part of the profits from the new coal excise was earmarked for the poor, and in 1656 meat forfeited by 'foreign' butchers was ordered to be given to the needy.[39]

The corporation administered the loan charities of Lady Judd (£100), John Hunwick (£300), and Thomas Ingram (£100),[40] which were used to set the poor on work, usually in spinning, carding, combing, and flax- or hemp-beating. Interest on the loans was applied to poor relief.[41] Poor children were apprenticed to trades- and craftsmen, often in exchange for the master's freedom of the town. In 1599 the keeper of the poorhouse was given the freedom in return for maintaining two poor girls;[42] the previous year William Ware had been admitted in return for keeping his parents from becoming a charge on the poor rate.[43]

The corporation ordered parish overseers to distrain the goods of those who refused to pay poor rates,[44] and Elizabeth, widow of Sir Thomas Lucas, appealed to the Privy Council in 1627 after the St. Giles's overseers had distrained a cow and calf for £3 rates.[45] When 23 inhabitants of All Saints' parish refused in 1629 to contribute to the relief of St. Botolph's poor, their churchwardens and overseers seem to have supported them, claiming to be unable to find any goods to distrain.[46] The corporation ordered additional assessments to be made in periods of particular need. In 1623, when high grain prices aggravated distress caused by depression in the new drapery trade, most inhabitants and occupiers of land in the town were ordered to be rated 'for 52 weeks over and above their weekly contribution'.[47]

Dearth and Depression

During the dearth of 1527 the 'substantial people' in Colchester were accused of stockpiling grain for themselves, and Cardinal Wolsey intervened to ensure that wheat in the town was actually sold to the inhabitants.[48] In 1551, another year of bad harvests, the Privy Council required the J.P.s of Kent to provide Colchester with 560 qr. of grain at reasonable prices.[49] In April 1563 the bailiffs and aldermen

35 Ibid. Boro. Mun., Acc. C1, Contribution Book to the Poor, unfoliated.
36 Ibid. D/B 5 Gb2, ff. 119v.–121v.; Gb3, ff, 62v.–63, 64, 81; Gb4, ff. 214, 229v.–230, 248; D/B 5 Cb1/10, f. 353; Cb1/11, f. 383; D/B 5 Cb2/13, f. 7; D/Y 2/2, p. 65.
37 Ibid. Boro. Mun., Acc. C1, Contribution Book to the Poor, unfoliated, end of vol.; ibid. D/B 5 Gb3, f. 162v.; for 'rawboots' above, this chapter, Econ. (Growth and Development).
38 E.R.O., D/B 5 Gb2, f. 163; ibid. Boro. Mun., Acc C.1, Contribution Book to the Poor, unfoliated, end of vol.
39 Ibid. D/B 5 Gb4, ff. 72, 150.
40 Ibid. D/B 5 Gb1, 1 Sept. 1590; 14 June 1591; 7 Aug. 1592; 18 June 1593; 10 Nov. 1595; Gb2, ff. 53v., 55; below, Charities.
41 E.R.O., D/B 5 Gb1, 14 June 1591; 7 Aug. 1592; 18 June 1593.
42 e.g. ibid. D/B 5 Cb1/6, f. 243; Cb2/6, ff. 222v., 249v.; Cb2/10, f. 51; D/B 5 Gb1, 1 Mar. 1599.
43 Ibid. D/B 5 Gb1, 19 Apr. 1598.
44 Ibid. D/B 5 Cb1/10, f. 82v.; Cb1/11, f. 107.
45 Ibid. D/B 5 Cb2/10, f. 240; Cal. S.P. Dom. 1627–8, 497.
46 E.R.O., D/Y 2/2, p. 41.
47 Ibid. D/B 5 Gb3, f. 31; D/B 5 Cb1/7, 221; B. Sharp, In Contempt of All Authority: Rural Artisans and Riot in West of Eng. 1586–1660, 25–6.
48 L. & P. Hen. VIII, iv (2), pp. 1629, 1781; Agric. Hist. Rev. xix. 152.
49 Acts of P.C. 1550–2, 329, 450; Agric. Hist. Rev. xix. 153; R. B. Outhwaite, Dearth, Public Policy and Social Disturbance in Eng. 1550–1800, 20.

took charge of the distribution of 500 qr. of grain brought from Danzig by alderman John Best, evidently in response to the bad harvest of the previous year.[50] In 1586, another year of dearth, the borough assembly levied a compulsory loan from the inhabitants to provide 400 qr. of Danzig rye.[51]

The years 1594–7 witnessed four successive bad harvests.[52] Between 1590 and 1593 the price of wheat averaged *c.* 23*s.* a quarter,[53] but by September 1594 it had risen to 42*s.* 10*d.*; it peaked at 48*s.* in November 1596 and remained at that level until August 1597.[54] Only in 1598 did the price fall back, to 32*s.* 6*d.* a quarter in October.[55] The response of the borough authorities was immediate. In November 1594 every alderman was ordered to lend £20, every first councillor £10, and every second councillor £5 for corn for the poor. In December a baker was appointed for each ward to bake three 'seams' of the town's grain for the poor. By May 1595 £408 had been collected and £380 spent on 289 qr. of grain; the small cash balance was distributed to the poor.[56] In December 1597 the bailiffs feared that many poor people would perish, in spite of the loan and of high poor rates which overburdened other townsmen, and in January 1598 Sir Robert Cecil allowed 400 qr. of grain to be shipped to Colchester from Norfolk despite the general restraint on the movement of corn.[57]

All that activity may not have been enough to prevent the poor from either starving or dying from disease induced by severe malnutrition. Although plague was not recorded, mortality reached double its average level in 1597 in four of the five parishes for which burial registers survive.[58] The poor parish of St. Botolph's was particularly severely affected, while St. James's, St. Leonard's, and St. Mary's-at-the-Walls also suffered. Numbers of deaths rose in July, and remained very high between September and December, a pattern at least compatible with a growing shortage of food towards the end of the harvest year 1596–7, capped by yet another bad harvest in 1597. The below-average number of baptisms in 1598 presumably reflects a shortfall in conceptions the previous year, perhaps induced by malnutrition and hence amenorrhea.[59] Furthermore, burials, particularly in St. Botolph's, fell sharply in January 1598, coinciding with the acquisition of grain from Norfolk.[60]

In other years the corporation's relief measures generally helped stave off such dire consequences.[61] The next period of severe difficulty started in 1629, when the bailiffs tried to prevent the export of 1,000 lasts of grain from Colchester because of the high local prices and the great number of poor in the town.[62] By December 1630 they were seeking to purchase rye in Norfolk for the poor with money lent or given, and in February 1631 they complained with effect to the Privy Council that local farmers, notably two Layer Breton yeomen, neglected to supply the town's market so that the poor were 'almost ready to famish and to commit outrages for want of corn'.[63] The harvest of 1630 was again very bad, the price of wheat and rye in Colchester rising to 46*s.* and 34*s.* a quarter respectively,[64] and the

[50] E.R.O., D/B 5 R5, f. 95v.; *Agric. Hist. Rev.* xix. 153; Outhwaite, *Dearth*, 20.
[51] E.R.O., D/B 5 Gb1, 12 Sept. 1586; *Cal. S.P. Dom.* 1581–90, 350; *Agric. Hist. Rev.* xix. 154; Outhwaite, *Dearth*, 20.
[52] *Agric. Hist. Rev.* xix. 154; Outhwaite, *Dearth*, 20.
[53] E.R.O., D/B 5 Cb1/3, ff. 200v., 348v.; D/B 5 Cr155, rot. 2d.
[54] Ibid. D/B 5 Cb1/4, ff. 40v., 134, 192v., 266v.
[55] Ibid. f. 340; D/B 5 Cb1/3, f.348v.; Cb1/4, f. 266v.
[56] Ibid. D/B 5 Gb1, 11 Nov., 2 Dec. 1594; 27 May 1595.
[57] Hist. MSS. Com. 9, *Salisbury,* vii. 526; *Acts of P.C.* 1597–8, 230–1.

[58] Goose, 'Econ. and Social Aspects', 306; P. Slack, *Impact of Plague in Tudor and Stuart Eng.* 73–6; A. B. Appleby, *Famine in Tudor and Stuart Eng.* 137–9; Outhwaite, *Dearth,* 29.
[59] Goose, 'Econ. and Social Aspects', 320; Appleby, *Famine,* 8–9.
[60] E.R.O., D/P 203/1/1, pp. 63–5.
[61] e.g. ibid. D/B 5 Gb2, f. 84.
[62] Ibid. D/Y 2/7, p. 247.
[63] Ibid. D/B 5 Gb3, f. 98; *Cal. S.P. Dom.* 1629–31, 500; *Acts of P.C.* 1630–1, 243.
[64] *Agric. Hist. Rev.* xix. 155; Outhwaite, *Dearth,* 20; E.R.O., D/B 5 Cb2/11, f. 143.

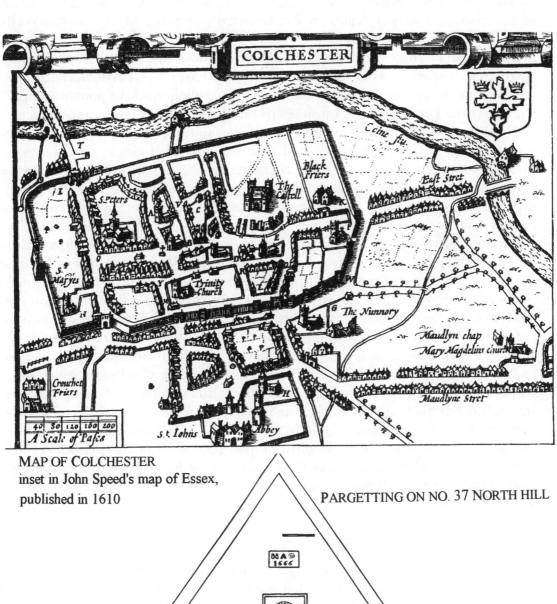

MAP OF COLCHESTER
inset in John Speed's map of Essex,
published in 1610

PARGETTING ON NO. 37 NORTH HILL

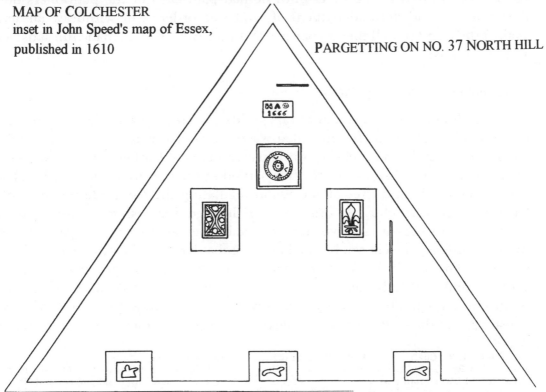

standard size of loaves of bread being reduced to that of the worst years of the 1590s.[65] Nevertheless plague rather than famine seems to have caused the doubling of the average mortality rates in St. Leonard's and St. Mary's-at-the-Walls in 1631.[66]

The dearth of 1630–1 was aggravated by the slump in the new drapery trade. In April 1631 it was reported that the suffering in Essex was particularly bad in the bay-making areas where the clothiers were not giving work to poor weavers.[67] In May 1631 the Privy Council, on the petition of 300 poor inhabitants of Colchester, ordered the bailiffs and aldermen to raise wages to their former level, or to provide a stock to set the poor on work, as had been done at Sudbury, or to take other measures to relieve the poor.[68] The Colchester authorities argued that raising wages would only reduce the amount of work given to the poor,[69] and the clothiers, ordered to raise wages by a sixth, replied that they could not provide employment even if they cut wages by a sixth.[70]

Further depression in the bay and say trade late in 1636 and in 1637 produced renewed controversy. Four weavers, claiming to speak for 2,000 others, petitioned the Privy Council against their low wages and troublesome work, alleging that many of them with their children were 'ready to perish'. Particular complaints were made against Thomas Reynolds, baymaker, for 'forcing them to take dead commodities such as they cannot put off'.[71] Reynolds had already, the previous January, been forced to recompense weavers to whom he had given overvalued says in lieu of wages. He denied the new charges, saying that he had given the men work and even lent them looms, and accusing three of them of being involved in burning down his house. Although he was supported by six Colchester clothworkers, the Privy Council concluded that he had oppressed and abused poor weavers. He was committed to the Fleet until he had paid each of the petitioners double the wages he had defrauded them of, and was ordered to withdraw all actions against them and pay all their expenses. Within a week he had made full satisfaction and was released.[72]

Economic and Social Regulation

In the absence of independent craft guilds the corporation played a major role in economic regulation. It controlled wages and set the assize of bread, and also appointed bakers' and butchers' wardens, searchers of leather, and overseers of the town lands. Trade disputes were often settled in the borough courts.[73] The Dutch had achieved a high degree of success in regulating the bay trade,[74] and from the later 16th century the corporation also devoted increasing attention to cloth production. In 1602 it established or re-established a weavers' company governed by two wardens, one chosen by the bailiffs and aldermen, the other by the freemen weavers. The wardens swore to ensure that all weavers performed their work skilfully and faithfully, and to enforce many of the provisions of the Statute of Artificers of 1563. The company laid down rules governing the length of apprenticeships, and the conditions of employment for journeymen, regulations repeated

[65] E.R.O., D/B 5 Cb2/11, f. 143; D/B 5 Cb1/4, ff. 192v., 266v.; D/B 5 R5, ff. 96v., 100 and v., 106, 109v.; D/B 5 Cr140, rot. 2d.; Cr141, rott. 7, 15.

[66] Goose, 'Econ. and Social Aspects', 306; E.R.O., D/P 245/1/1; D/P 246/1/1.

[67] Sharp, In Contempt, 30.

[68] Acts of P.C. 1630–1, 358–9.

[69] Cal. S.P. Dom. 1625–49, 430.

[70] W. Hunt, Puritan Movement: Coming of Revolution in an Eng. County, 244.

[71] P.R.O., PC 2/47, ff. 389–90; Cal. S.P. Dom. 1637, 32, 44.

[72] Cal. S.P. Dom. 1637, 44, 87–9, 115; P.R.O., PC 2/47, ff. 390, 422.

[73] E.R.O., D/B 5 Cr82–186; D/B 5 Cb1/2–24; D/B 5 Cb2/3–34.

[74] Immigrants and Minorities, i. 266–7; above, this chapter, Econ. (Growth and Development).

in 1608 and 1609.[75] In 1618 a company of English bay and saymakers was established, parallel to the Dutch company, for the reform of 'deceits and abuses' in the craft.[76] Among other matters the new company was required to regulate wages and impose reasonable rates, and was apparently doing so more assiduously than the Dutch company in 1622.[77]

The weavers' and other trade ordinances discriminated against 'foreigners', as did the borough authorities. Despite the welcome extended to the Dutch settlers in 1565,[78] it was ordered in 1580 that no more Dutch be allowed to settle without the consent of the bailiffs and aldermen. In 1584 householders were forbidden to receive tenants likely to prove a charge on the town, and in 1591 they were forbidden to let houses or rooms to anyone who had not lived in the town for three years or else given two sureties of £20. The constables were ordered to eject recent immigrants from employment and put longer-term residents in their places, and to remove from the town all the poor who had been there for less than three years.[79] The corporation claimed in 1613 that the increasing number of 'incomers' was the main cause of the rising numbers of poor, and in 1622 that the failure to exclude immigrants was the principal cause of the great poverty in the town.[80] Restrictions on immigrants continued in force into the 1630s.[81] In 1637 the corporation attempted to protect the interests of those who had been born free or served long apprenticeships by raising the fine for purchasing the freedom to £10, and requiring the consent of six free burgesses of the same trade to the admission.[82]

Nevertheless considerable numbers of people settled in Colchester in the late 16th and early 17th centuries, enough to sustain a population growth well above that obtainable by natural increase.[83] On average 150 migrants were apprenticed in Colchester each decade between c. 1580 and 1630. Of the 1,014 apprentices whose indentures record their place of origin (Table VII),[84] a quarter came from Colchester itself, a further third from elsewhere in Essex and a fifth from Suffolk. Less than a fifth came from outside East Anglia, mainly from the south midlands, particularly the cloth-working areas of Cambridgeshire. Trading contacts with south and east coast ports probably account for the c. 5 per cent of apprentices from the east midlands, the south, and the south-east. Very few came from the more westerly regions of the country.

Burgess admissions similarly record predominantly short-range migration and a distinct bias towards the east coast of England among those moving longer distances. Birthplaces can be identified for 1,425 of 1,500 men admitted in the 16th and early 17th centuries.[85] Of those, 435 (30.5 per cent) were born in Colchester, a further 386 (27.1 per cent) elsewhere in Essex, and 232 (16.3 per cent) in Suffolk. Significant numbers came from Yorkshire (46), Norfolk (31), London and Middlesex (26), Cambridgeshire (21), Kent (21), Lincolnshire (18), Hertfordshire (15), Lancashire (13), Buckinghamshire (12), Staffordshire (11), and Northumberland (10). Thirty-five were born overseas.

Migrants arriving to take up apprenticeships or to purchase the freedom stood

[75] E.R.O., D/B 5 Gb2, ff. 23–24v., 74, 82–3.
[76] P.R.O., SP 14/115, no. 28; Cal. S.P. Dom. 1611–18, 550; Univ. Birmingham Hist. Jnl. vii. 49.
[77] P.R.O., SP 14/129, no. 70 (1).
[78] Above, this chapter, Econ. (Growth and Development).
[79] E.R.O., D/B 5 Gb1, 17 Oct. 1580; 17 Mar. 1584; 17 June 1591.
[80] Ibid. D/B 5 Gb3, f. 172 and v.
[81] Ibid. D/B 5 Gb2, 23–24v., 74, 82–3, 157; Gb3, ff. 13v.,

83 and v., 157v.–158, 169v.–180.
[82] Ibid. D/B 5 Gb2, ff. 119v.–121; Gb3, ff. 14–16v.
[83] Goose, 'Econ. and Social Aspects', 266–7; above, this chapter, Intro.
[84] E.R.O., D/B 5 Cr142–86; D/B 5 Cb1/2–9; D/B 5 Cb2/3–11; D/B 5 Gb1–3. All but a handful fall between the years 1580 and 1630.
[85] E.R.O., D/B 5 Cr82–186; D/B 5 Cb1/2–9; D/B 5 Cb2/3–11; D/B 5 Gb1–3.

at the more respectable end of the social spectrum. Others less respectable and less welcome also found their way to Colchester. Many such vagrants had come from other towns, and a high proportion of them had travelled considerable distances. Of the 236 predominantly single men or women apprehended in and expelled from the town between 1630 and 1664 whose place of origin is known, a little over 28 per cent had moved over 100 miles, while over 70 per cent had moved more than 40 miles. Only 88 (37.3 per cent) came from East Anglia, 42 (17.8 per cent) from London and Middlesex, and as many as 20 (8.5 per cent) from Ireland. The dearth

TABLE VII: ORIGINS OF COLCHESTER APPRENTICES *c.* 1580–1630

	Number	per cent
Colchester	258	25.6
Essex (other)	358	35.6
Suffolk	196	19.5
Norfolk	13	1.3
Total East Anglia	825	82.0
Cambridgeshire	57	5.7
Hertfordshire	12	1.2
Huntingdonshire	14	1.4
Total South Midlands	96	9.5
Lincolnshire	18	1.8
Total East Midlands	28	2.8
Middlesex (including London)	12	1.2
Total South and South-East	26	2.6
Total North	19	1.9
Total South-West	7	0.7
Total West Midlands	3	0.3
Total Other	2	0.2
TOTAL	1,006	100.0

Note: Regional groupings as follows:
East Anglia: Essex, Suff., Norf.
South Midlands: Beds., Bucks., Cambs., Herts., Hunts., Northants., Oxon.
East Midlands: Derb., Leics., Lincs., Notts., Rut.
South and South-East: Berks., Hants, Kent, Mdx., Surr., Suss.
North: Ches., Cumb., co. Dur., Lancs., Northumb., Yorks., Westmld.
South-West: Cornw., Devon, Dors., Som., Wilts.
West Midlands: Glos., Herefs., Mon., Salop., Staffs., Warws., Worcs.
Other: Ireland, Scotland, Wales, Overseas.

Only counties from which 10 or more apprentices came to Colchester are
listed separately.

Sources: E.R.O., D/B 5 Cb1/2–9; Cb2/3–11.

years 1630 and 1631 produced particularly large numbers of long distance immigrants.[86]

The whipping and expulsion of vagrants was only one part of an often punitive policy towards the poor. Alehouses were attacked in 1598 as 'harbourers of thieves, harlots, and other lewd persons' and blamed for beastliness and drunkenness which was 'the utter undoing' of many poor people.[87] Alehouse keepers, like Thomas Wilson in 1601, had to swear to prohibit cards, dice, and other unlawful games, not to permit drunkenness, and to forbid all drinking during the times of church services. They were to sell food and drink only to legitimate wayfarers or to the poorer sort of townsmen, to take no lodgers for more than a day and a night unless they could vouch for them, to control the sale of goods in their houses, and to admit the constables and other officers at all times.[88] The town was well supplied with inns and alehouses: 7 innkeepers and 69 tipplers were recorded in 1574, and 5 taverners, 5 innkeepers, and 38 alehouse keepers in 1577.[89] In 1613 the borough ordered a reduction in the number of alehouses and stricter vetting of their keepers to keep out 'incomers' and to suppress idleness,[90] but in 1686 the town was second only to Chelmsford in the county in the number of beds (198) available in its inns, and there were still at least 31 inns or alehouses in 1705.[91]

Begging by any but the 'very lame and aged not able to work' had been prohibited in 1591. Six years later an overseer and a beadle, paid for by an additional poor rate, were appointed to prevent able-bodied men from begging.[92] From 1622 four beadles were appointed to seek out unlicensed beggars, and to control the licensed ones, who were to be confined to particular parishes.[93] In 1613 a new workhouse was founded to employ the poor, lame, and impotent.[94] It was governed by four aldermen and sixteen common councillors who appointed other officers to punish and order the idle persons brought there. The new institution was clearly both workhouse and house of correction. Indeed, it was regularly called the house of correction, and its inmates included men like the Norfolk tailor committed in 1636 for drunkenness and swearing and for abusing the high constable. In 1622 detailed regulations were made for providing work for the more respectable poor in their own homes.[95]

Between 1622 and 1639 the clerk entered in the register the condition or occupation of many of those buried in St. Botolph's parish.[96] Poverty was widespread. Of the 11 people buried in June 1622, for instance, 6, including 3 widows, were 'poor' and 1 'very poor'. Many of those buried were described as weavers or 'poor weavers', a substantial number were Dutch, and a few were vagrants. The high proportion of children among them may be further evidence of poverty. By the later 17th century there appears to have been less official concern about poverty. The problem had apparently been relieved by the stabilization of population and prices and the reduction in immigration, combined with the continued growth of the town's economy.[97] The substantial increase in 'rawboots'

[86] *Migration and Society in Early Modern Eng.* ed. P. Clark and D. Souden, 49–76; cf. *Crisis and Order in Eng. Towns 1500–1700.* [87] E.R.O., D/B 5 Gb1, 12 Dec. 1598.
[88] Ibid. Boro. Mun., Tradesmen's Recogs. 1599–1605, ff. 13v.–14.
[89] Ibid: D/B 5 Sb2/2, ff. 1–20v.; F. G. Emmison, *Elizabethan Life: Disorder,* 215.
[90] E.R.O., D/B 5 Gb2, ff. 119–121v.
[91] Ibid. D/B 5 Sr76, rott. 7–9; W. J. Petchey, *Prospect of Maldon,* 138.
[92] E.R.O., D/B 5 Gb1, 14 June 1591; 18 Nov. 1597.
[93] Ibid. D/B 5 Gb3, f. 16 and v.

[94] Ibid. D/Y 2/2, p. 60; D/B 5 Gb1, 1 Mar. 1599; Gb2, ff. 119–121v.
[95] Ibid. D/B 5 Sb1/4, 11 July 1636; D/B 5 Gb2, ff. 130v., 161; Gb3, ff. 14–16v.; Gb4, ff. 100, 174; Gb5, f. 313; Gb6, p. 70; below, Mun. Bldgs. (Prison).
[96] E.R.O., D/P 203/1/1.
[97] Ibid. D/B 5 Gb2–6; E. A. Wrigley and R. S. Schofield, *Population Hist. Eng. 1541–1871: a Reconstruction,* 210–11; *Past and Present,* lxxxiii. 81–3; R. B. Outhwaite, *Inflation in Tudor and Early Stuart Eng.* 14; above, this chapter, Intro.; Econ. (Growth and Development).

CHARLES II'S CHARTER, 1684

TABLE VIII: TAXED AND EXEMPT HOUSEHOLDS IN COLCHESTER 1674

Parish	Taxed	Exempt	Total	per cent Exempt
St. Botolph	116	204	320	63.8
St. Giles	100	194	294	66.0
St. James	106	155	261	59.4
St. Peter	163	88	251	35.1
St. Mary-at-the-Walls	103	92	195	47.2
St. Nicholas	78	77	155	49.7
St. Leonard	70	83	153	54.2
St. Martin	70	42	112	37.5
Lexden	33	64	97	66.0
All Saints	60	22	82	26.8
Greenstead	26	40	66	60.6
St. Mary Magdalen	17	41	58	70.7
St. Runwald	40	13	53	24.5
Mile End	21	30	51	58.8
Holy Trinity	35	16*	51	31.4
West Donyland	10	–	10	–
Total	1,048	1,161	2,209	52.6

* All those exempt in West Donyland were paupers, needing no exemption certificate, and hence not included with the exempt.

Source: P.R.O., E 179/246/22.

as bay manufacturing expanded presumably helped to alleviate poverty, but special relief payments were necessary on several occasions. By 1678 the declining Dutch community was having considerable difficulty in maintaining its poor, as it had agreed to do when it was first established.[98] At the close of the 17th century Colchester petitioned parliament for the establishment of a new workhouse to cope with the increasing numbers of poor, to prevent idleness and disorders among the 'meaner' people, and to reduce the burden of the poor rate. An Act of 1698 authorized the establishment in the town of a workhouse under the control of a corporation of the poor.[99]

Social Structure in the Later 17th Century

The hearth tax return of 1674 (Tables VIII and IX), indicates that 53 per cent of households were too poor to be taxed. To those must be added a figure, c. 10 per cent of the population, for the paupers who were omitted from the returns, making altogether 1,406 households, or 57 per cent of the total.[1] The base of the social pyramid, the poor or relatively poor, was a broad one, broader than that found in most other provincial towns.[2] That reflects the town's economic structure, for the poverty of many weavers and other workers in the labour-intensive cloth

[98] E.R.O., D/B 5 Gb5, ff. 133, 153, 175, 213v., 352v., 364; D/B 5 Sb3/1, pp. 3, 8, 19, 42–4, 46–7, 119; Cal. S.P. Dom. 1683–4, 258.
[99] E.R.O., D/Y 2/2, pp. 61–4; D/B 5 Gb6, pp. 146, 200; ibid. Q/SR 554/8; C.J. xii. 165–6, 207, 263, 265, 273; P. Slack, Eng. Poor Law 1531–1782, 46; 9 & 10 Wm. III, c. 37 (Priv. Act).
[1] Goose, 'Econ. and Social Aspects', 325–7, 339.

[2] W. G. Hoskins, Industry, Trade and People in Exeter (1968), 117; Suff. in 1674, ed. S. A. H. Hervey, 52; V.C.H. Yorks. E.R. i. 161; R. Howell, Newcastle Upon Tyne and the Puritan Revolution, 350–1; Salop. Hearth Tax Roll 1672, ed. W. Watkins-Pitchford; Jnl. of Chester and North Wales Archit. Arch. and Hist. Soc. xxxvi. 31; V.C.H. Leics. iv. 156–9; Goose, 'Econ. and Social Aspects', 338–42.

industry was amply attested by contemporaries, and the Essex textile areas all exhibited relatively high proportions of people exempt from hearth tax.[3] The high proportion of small or exempt households in St. Botolph's and St. Giles's parishes is explained by the number of weavers there: of 109 weavers and clothworkers identified in the town in the period 1620–99 as many as 47 (43 per cent) lived in

TABLE IX: HOUSEHOLDS OF DIFFERENT SIZES IN COLCHESTER, 1674

	1 Hearth		2 Hearths		3–5 Hearths		6–9 Hearths		10+ Hearths		Total
	no.	per cent	no.	per cent	no.	per cent	no.	per cent	no.	per cent	
St. Botolph	152	47.5	98	30.6	51	15.9	15	4.7	4	1.3	320
St. Giles	186	63.3	79	26.9	22	7.5	7	2.4	–	–	294
St. James	133	51.0	59	22.6	45	17.2	20	7.7	4	1.5	261
St. Peter	86	34.3	55	21.9	89	35.5	16	6.4	5	2.0	251
St. Mary-W.	72	36.9	69	35.4	37	19.0	14	7.2	3	1.5	195
St. Nicholas	67	43.2	39	25.2	34	21.9	12	7.7	3	1.9	155
St. Leonard	52	34.0	56	36.6	31	20.3	11	7.2	3	2.0	153
St. Martin	44	39.3	32	28.6	31	27.7	4	3.6	1	0.9	112
Lexden	56	57.7	14	14.4	21	21.6	6	6.2	–	–	97
All Saints	21	25.6	21	25.6	30	36.6	8	9.8	2	2.4	82
Greenstead	37	56.1	15	22.7	13	19.7	1	1.5	–	–	66
St. Mary M.	45	77.6	6	10.3	6	10.3	1	1.7	–	–	58
St. Runwald	5	9.4	15	28.3	22	41.5	9	17.0	2	3.8	53
Mile End	31	60.8	11	21.6	9	17.6	–	–	–	–	51
Holy Trinity	16	31.4	16	31.4	11	21.6	6	11.8	2	3.9	51
West Donyland	3	30.0	3	30.0	2	20.0	–	–	2	20.0	10
Total	1,006	45.5	588	26.6	454	20.6	130	5.9	31	1.4	2,209

Source: P.R.O., E 179/246/22.

those two parishes.[4] St. Giles's and St. Botolph's also received the largest abatements for poverty, £6 7s. and £5 15s. respectively, in Colchester in the poll tax of 1667.[5]

The funds generated by a labour-intensive industry were produced at the cost of the depression of a large section of the urban labour force. The figures reflect the impact of population growth and inflation throughout the 16th century and the early 17th, and possibly also the development of increasingly capitalistic methods of production, the decline of the independent weaver or small clothier, and a growth in the numbers of dependent textile wage workers. The corporation attempted to limit the size of units of production, in 1613, for instance, prohibiting the employment of more than five weavers, or the use of more than two broad looms and one narrow or three narrow looms and one broad. Its failure to halt the trend is demonstrated by the claims of Thomas Reynolds and others in the 1630s to employ large numbers of hands, and by the distress of many workers during the textile slumps of the 1620s and 1630s.[6]

At the other end of the social scale economic development generated considerable wealth. In 1674 c. 7 per cent of those assessed for hearth tax lived in households

[3] E. Kerridge, Textile Manufactures in Early Modern Eng. 206; Burley, 'Econ. Development of Essex', 339–44, 361; Supple, Commercial Crisis, 8–14; Textile Hist. and Econ. Hist. ed. N. B. Harte and K. G. Ponting, 3.

[4] Goose, 'Econ. and Social Aspects', 223.

[5] E.R.O., D/Y 2/2, loose material.

[6] Ibid. D/B 5 Gb2, f. 121 and v.; G. Unwin, Studies in Econ. Hist. 272, 281, 292; D. C. Coleman, Ind. in Tudor and Stuart Eng. 29; Sharp, In Contempt of All Authority, 7, 259–60; above, this chapter, Econ. (Growth and Development).

with 6 or more hearths, and there was a distinct contrast between the poorer suburban parishes, like St. Giles's and St. Botolph's, and the central and wealthy St. Runwald's, where over 20 per cent of households fell into that category. Of the 9 heads of household with 10 or more hearths whose occupations can be traced, 5 were merchants, 2 were bay- or saymakers, 1 was a joiner, and 1 an innholder. Twenty-six occupiers of dwellings with 6–9 hearths could be identified by occupation. Eleven were bay- or saymakers, and 3 were merchants; the only other occupation to feature twice was that of brewer. As in the 1520s, cloth production and mercantile activity were the main, though not the only, avenues to prosperity in the town.

Some members of the Dutch community amassed substantial wealth from the new draperies which they had introduced. Francis Hockee in 1638 bequeathed a total of £660 in cash to his children, while Francis Pollard left over £520 cash in 1630, and another Francis Pollard, saymaker, left well over £1,000 in 1670. In 1687 Andrew Fromanteel devised a number of houses in Colchester, besides lands at Frating, Great or Little Bentley, and Stanway (Essex), at Aldham, Hadleigh, and Stratford (Suff.), and at Bennington and Boston (Lincs.). George Tayspill, saymaker, bequeathed over £3,000 in money in 1666, and the Tayspill family became one of the wealthiest and most important in the town.[7]

The profits of saymaking were not confined to the Dutch. William Johnson bequeathed £1,400 in cash in 1634, besides the 'competent estate' he had already settled upon his son William. In 1652 Robert Smith, baymaker, left £800 to two of his children, and £30 a year to his wife from his lands and houses in St. James's parish, and in Copford and Birch. Henry Franklin, another baymaker, in 1683 made bequests of over £1,300 in cash and devised houses and land in All Saints' parish and in Wimbish, Thaxted, Lamarsh, Alphamstone, Thorpe-le-Soken, and Tendring. Drapers also prospered; Ralph Creffield the elder in 1666, having already provided for two daughters, bequeathed £700 cash, and lands and houses in St. Peter's, St. James's, and St. Botolph's, and in Great and Little Wigborough, Elmstead, Alresford, Frating, Thorrington, and Great Bentley. Two years later Edmund Thurston of St. Runwald's, draper, left cash bequests totalling over £2,600 to his wife and children, besides his land and houses in Colchester and in Dedham, Great Horkesley, Colne Engaine, Thorpe-le-Soken, Little Holland, St. Osyth, Fingringhoe, Wix, and Walton, and in Stoke-by-Nayland (Suff.).[8]

Among the other later 17th-century tradesmen and craftsmen to leave several hundred pounds, usually in addition to both town and rural land, were a vintner, a brewer, a maltster, a coalmerchant, an ironmonger, a cutler, a carpenter, a cooper, and a tanner. As early as 1624 Geoffrey Langley, grocer, bequeathed almost £1,000 in cash besides an impressive landed estate in Colchester and elsewhere. In 1686 John Furley the elder, merchant, bequeathed over £2,000 in cash, and land in Essex, and houses in Holy Trinity and at the Hythe. In 1696 Isaac Shirley left £1,000 and his lands and houses to his four children, and in 1698 William Talcott of All Saints', whose daughter Ann had married into the Furley family, left enough land, including an 117-a. wood at Stanway and an 111-a. one at East Donyland, to underwrite bequests of £80 a year besides c. £1,000 in cash.[9]

7 E.R.O., D/ABW 55/49; D/ACW 11/188; P.R.O., PROB 11/320, f. 136; PROB 11/333, f. 446; PROB 11/388, f. 287; *Immigrants and Minorities*, i. 271; *Proc. Hug. Soc.* xxi. 24.

8 E.R.O., D/ACW 17/180; D/ACR 8/58; P.R.O., PROB 11/166, f. 152v.; PROB 11/223, f. 226; PROB 11/373, f. 143.

9 P.R.O., PROB 11/382, f. 233; PROB 11/430, f. 161v.; PROB 11/444, f. 59.

By the later 17th century several men described themselves as gentleman or esquire. Some were still clearly engaged in trade, like Henry Lamb esquire who in 1688 bequeathed his three ships, *Anne*, *Abigail and Thomas*, and *Resolution*, besides houses in St. Runwald's, St. Martin's, St. Giles's, and St. Nicholas's and over £1,200 in cash. Others may have retired from trade or have been country landowners attracted to the town by the lure of urban society. Such urban gentlemen often exhibited considerable wealth. In 1690 Joseph Thurston, probably a descendant of Thomas Thurston woollendraper and alderman, bequeathed over £3,400 in cash as well as a large urban and rural estate. Ralph Harrison of St. Leonard's left over £2,000 in cash in 1655, and Thomas Reynolds of St. James's over £3,500 in 1665; both were aldermen and gentlemen and both also owned lands and houses.[10]

The resilience of the town's economy was demonstrated by its rapid recovery from the siege of 1648 and from the plague of 1665–6.[11] Despite the recent expense of caring for its own sick poor, in October 1666 Colchester collected £103 8s. 9d. for the relief of London after the Great Fire.[12] Although by the late 17th century borough finances were precarious, with indebtedness preventing the construction of a new fishmarket in 1687,[13] the town was able to tap into the wealth of its leading citizens, and also to take advantage of an asset that had been a key to its economic success for over 100 years, when it mortgaged the Dutch Bay Hall and its profits besides the borough lands to wealthy burgesses.[14]

Social Disturbance

Seventeenth-century Colchester witnessed the simultaneous growth of wealth and poverty, and the development of political and religious factions, its inhabitants being called a factious multitude by the bishop of London's commissary in 1623,[15] but the urban social fabric held together remarkably well. In the early 1640s, however, religious and political differences were aggravated by economic distress as the cloth trade, which had been sluggish for 18 months, ground to a halt in 1642. There was a spate of petitions to parliament from Colchester and other towns and counties. Rumours grew of profiteering by the town's M.P., Harbottle Grimston, while the weavers spread the view that M.P.s only sat 'for their own ends to enrich themselves'.[16] Such grievances fuelled the flames of the Civil War factions.[17]

On occasion purely economic grievances did lead to riots, but such disturbances were infrequent. In 1538 some 23 Colchester men had been involved in an inclosure riot.[18] Two inclosure disturbances broke out in 1603, one said to involve 100 people, the other 400. Pales, posts, and rails on St. John's green were pulled down, possibly with the encouragement of Sir Thomas Lucas, who maintained that the pales encroached on the green.[19] More immediately related to the condition of the urban economy was the abortive rising of under-employed weavers in 1566.[20] There is little evidence of rioting in the town in the earlier 17th century, despite recurrent hardship resulting from harvest failure and depression of the cloth trade.[21]

[10] E.R.O., D/ABR 7/290; D/ABR 11/308; P.R.O., PROB 11/144, f. 115; PROB 11/247, f. 146v.; PROB 11/316, f. 382; PROB 11/320, f. 33; PROB 11/330, f. 35v.; PROB 11/332, f. 224; PROB 11/358, f. 13v.; PROB 11/391, f. 153v.; PROB 11/395, f. 84; PROB 11/400, f. 318; PROB 11/401, f. 295; PROB 11/408, f. 299v.; PROB 11/429, f. 184v.

[11] Above, this chapter, Intro.

[12] E.R.O., D/B 5 Gb4, f. 356v.

[13] Ibid. D/B 5 Gb5, f. 264.

[14] Ibid. D/B 5 Gb6, pp. 13, 237, 345, 436.

[15] Hunt, *Puritan Movement*, 94, 104, 176.

[16] A. Fletcher, *Outbreak of Eng. Civil War*, 223, 294.

[17] Above, this chapter, Intro.

[18] E.R.O., D/B 5 Cr107, rot. 3 and d.

[19] Ibid. D/B 5 Sb2/6, ff. 92v.–93.

[20] Above, this chapter, Econ. (Readjustment and Recovery).

[21] Sharpe, *Crime*, 136.

It was in the later 17th century, when conditions for the lower classes were generally improving and economic pressures decreasing, that the borough's textile workers next flexed their muscles.[22] In 1667 the people of St. Giles's attacked the commissioners for the collection of the hearth tax, pursuing them to the King's Head inn where the J.P.s were sitting.[23] In 1675 as many as 300 or 400 poor weavers, summoned by a horn, assembled at 2 a.m. in St. Mary's churchyard, marched to St. John's fields, where the mayor and officers failed to placate them, and thence through the town to John Furley's house, which they threatened to plunder and pull down. Their main demand was for better wages for bay weaving, although Furley's particular crime was 'selling corn out of the land'. With the help of some townsmen the rioters were eventually dispersed, but the trained bands were raised and kept on the alert for three weeks.[24]

Four years later, in 1679, a great company apparently marched through town 'in a rude and tumultuous manner' led by a man with colours flying,[25] and further rumblings were heard in the 1690s after a succession of bad harvests.[26] There were riots in April 1693, a year in which disturbances occurred in a number of towns upon rumour that corn was being bought up and exported to France.[27] In 1695–6 the borough paid for taking four rioters to Chelmsford.[28] In 1703 ten men rioted at the stocks at Lexden; like the rioters of 1675 they had been summoned by a horn, suggesting that the apparently minor affair might have developed into a more general protest.[29] In the early 18th century more serious disturbances arose from depression in the cloth trade and the consequent fall in wages. In 1711 two men declared that all baymakers who would not pay weavers 10s. a bay should be pulled from their beds by the poor, carried to St. John's fields, and there hung up.[30] Matters came to a head in 1715 when an assembly of 700–800 weavers stopped proceedings at the Dutch Bay Hall and effectively paralysed both government and industry in the town for three weeks.[31]

The town had weathered earlier trade slumps and poor harvests without such outbreaks of violence. It was some time before the decline of the high real wages of the early 16th century caused distress,[32] and the expansion of the textile industry after the arrival of the Dutch had shielded the town from the worst effects of trade slumps.[33] Even in years of dearth, coarse grain and fish such as sprats, 'the weavers' beef', were usually affordable,[34] and in difficult years the borough authorities were able to do enough to alleviate the short-term problem and to show their concern for the welfare of the poor.[35] By the early 18th century, however, the bay trade had started to contract, organized social protest was more common, and the borough authorities had lost some of their power to regulate the town's economy in the interests of social stability. Fewer foreigners were willing to purchase the freedom, preferring to risk fines for 'keeping open shop' in the borough.[36] The sale of the freedom for political or financial ends can only have tended to discredit the corporation.[37] In 1698 the bakers were accused of conspiring to defraud the poor by counting only 12 instead of 13 or 14 to the dozen, and other traders of

[22] Wrigley and Schofield, *Population Hist.* 210–11; C. G. A. Clay, *Econ. Expansion and Social Change: Eng. 1500–1700*, i. 140–1.

[23] E.R.O., D/B 5 Sb2/9, f. 166.

[24] Ibid. D/B 5 Sb2/9, ff. 223v.–226v.; P.R.O., PC 2/65, ff. 17, 20; *Cal. S.P. Dom.* 1675–6, 513–14.

[25] E.R.O., D/B 5 Sb2/9, f. 245.

[26] *Agric. Hist. Rev.* xvi. 30; Outhwaite, *Dearth*, 20.

[27] E.R.O., D/B 5 Sr56, rot. 13; P.R.O., PC 2/75, f. 146.

[28] E.R.O., D/B 5 Aa1/35, f. 67.

[29] Ibid. D/B 5 Sr71, rot. 13.

[30] Ibid. D/B 5 Sr91, rot. 12.

[31] *Bull. Inst. Hist. Res.* xxix. 220–30; Sharpe, *Crime*, 137–8.

[32] *Immigrants and Minorities*, i. 269–72.

[33] E.R.O., D/B 5 Sb2/6, f. 270.

[34] Ibid. D/B 5 Cb1/4, f. 340; T. Fuller, *Worthies of Eng.* i. 498.

[35] *Past and Present*, lxxi. 22–42.

[36] E.R.O., D/B 5 Gb6, pp. 112, 116; D/B 5 Sr62, rot. 59.

[37] Below, this chapter, Boro. Govt.

forestalling butter and eggs before they reached the market. Critics asked for the public display of the assize of bread so that the poor should know what they ought to have for their money.[38] In 1712 several bakers who had been punished for breaking the assize sued the mayor and aldermen.[39] That antagonism between rulers and ruled, rich and poor, contrasts with the paternalism of Thomas Christmas's will in 1520,[40] and illustrates the distance which separated early 18th-century Colchester society from that which had existed two centuries earlier.

TOPOGRAPHY

The Town to 1640

By c. 1500 houses extended well beyond the town walls in ribbon developments along the major roads, notably East Hill and East Street, Middleborough and North Street, and Magdalen Street, and in more compact suburbs outside South gate and Head gate. The settlement at the Hythe was still separated from the town by fields. Within the walls large areas of open ground remained, notably at Bury field in the south-east quarter, around the castle in the north-east, and between the wall and Head Street and North Hill in the west. Even in the main streets a decline in population in the later Middle Ages had reduced the pressure on space, and most houses had gardens or yards. Physical decay, particularly in the northern and south-eastern suburbs, seems to have become noticeable by the 1520s and 1530s, and the dissolution of the monasteries hastened the decline of the south-eastern suburb, which had been dominated by St. John's abbey and St. Botolph's priory.

By 1535 four cottages in Magdalen Street had fallen down, and an empty house site in the same street was recorded in 1538.[41] By 1539, of the houses owing rents to St. John's abbey, two in Stanwell Street and two in Lodder's Lane (Abbeygate Street) were 'decayed', and another, possibly in East Stockwell Street, had been knocked down, but the total of five houses was relatively insignificant in a rental of c. 163.[42] A house and three 'rents', small houses or cottages, at the Hythe were made into one house before 1542.[43] Before 1543 a total of 29 houses in Head ward, at least nine of them within the walls, had either been taken down or were 'sore decayed',[44] but not all were necessarily dwellings. As many as 13 houses formerly belonging to St. John's south and east of the walls had fallen down or been destroyed by c. 1550: 2 in Magdalen Street, 1 in Stanwell Street, 4 in Lodders Lane, at least 3 on St. John's green, 2 in East Street, and 1 in Holy Trinity parish, probably outside Scheregate. Another 34 were in need of repair. Not all the 'decay' was recent; three houses in Lodders Lane had been 'badly devastated' for 16 years, and that in Holy Trinity parish had been totally destroyed 'for a long time'. The decay of a house in East Street and of the Lamb or New inn on St. John's green was attributed to the attainder of the abbey in 1539.[45]

Two houses beyond North bridge had been made into one by 1534, and two in Wyre Street were similarly joined in 1540. Buildings on a plot in Stockwell Street, apparently developed late in the Middle Ages, had fallen down by 1541.[46] A house called Hell, on the south side of Culver Street, seems to have been demolished

[38] E.R.O., D/B 5 Sr62, rot. 17.
[39] Ibid. D/B 5 Gb7, ff. 9, 10.
[40] P.R.O., PROB 11/19, ff. 28 sqq.; above, this chapter, Econ. (Early 16th century).
[41] E.R.O., D/B 5 Cr104, rot. 6d.; Cr106, rot. 5.
[42] P.R.O., SC 6/Hen. VIII/976.
[43] E.R.O., D/B 5 Cr113, rot. 17.   [44] Ibid. D/Y 2/2, p. 13.
[45] P.R.O., E 310/13/40; E 318/20/1054.
[46] E.R.O., D/B 5 Cr104, rot. 9; D/B 5 Cr110, rot. 4d.; D/B 5 Cr113, rot. 18d.

between 1540 and 1543.[47] In 1548–9 the borough chamberlain was unable to collect rents from unoccupied houses outside Ryegate, in Bere Lane (Vineyard Street), and next to Holy Trinity church, while a house in East Street had fallen down.[48] There were still at least 2 empty plots, formerly house sites, in Stanwell Street, 1 in Lodders Lane, and 3 on St. John's green in 1581.[49]

Elsewhere there is evidence for increased occupancy and some new building or rebuilding. A house in St. Botolph's parish, divided in 1503, remained so in 1549, and ownership of part of a house there was disputed c. 1530.[50] Part of a large house in St. Peter's parish was sold in 1543, and Thomas Whitbread (d. c. 1520) divided a house in Headgate into two. A large house in West Stockwell Street seems to have been divided in 1532.[51] In 1542 the former St. Botolph's priory barn near the corner of St. Botolph's Street and Magdalen Street was converted into houses, and other parts of the St. Botolph's site developed.[52] In 1548–9 the chamberlain collected rents from 'newly built' shops and solars in front of the Red Lion inn and from 'new' buildings in Maidenburgh Street behind the George inn.[53]

When the economy began to recover in the 1550s or 1560s,[54] physical repair and expansion soon followed. In 1578 the borough required the tenant of a house west of the moot hall to rebuild the parts of it which had fallen down.[55] In 1580 alderman Robert Mott sold a house 'lately waste and recently built' in St. Martin's parish. At least one plot of land taken from Bury field had been 'lately' built on in 1581. A newly built house on the corner of North Street and Sheepen Lane was sold in 1594.[56] In 1610 the borough granted a building lease of a piece of waste in St. James's parish, and licensed building on the waste in East Stockwell Street.[57] Another building lease, of land at the Hythe, was granted in 1608, and in 1609 Henry Barrington agreed to build a new millhouse there with a cellar, a brick chimney, and two fireplaces. In 1623 the water bailiff was instructed to demolish and rebuild the warehouses on the waterfront.[58] Two new houses were built next to a house in All Saints' parish between 1559 and 1621. By 1634 the adjoining barn had been made into a cottage, and that too was divided in 1635.[59] The former no. 11 Sir Isaac's Walk may also have been converted to a dwelling-house from a barn at that time. It stands well back from the street frontage, and its plan, with three rooms on each floor and a large internal stack, is like that of a farmhouse. Before 1625 two 'rents' and a house were built in Dovehouse field on the west side of the road beyond North bridge, and the borough granted a building lease of a large plot outside Headgate in 1619.[60]

Division of houses continued: a house called the Crown, on the south side of High Street next to the Red Lion inn, had been divided into two before 1555, and in 1597 it was occupied by four households.[61] William Ingram in 1601 and 1603 sold two separate parcels of his house in Wyre Street, which itself seems once to have been part of the neighbouring house. By 1622 a house in All Saints' parish was divided between three or four tenants, some apparently occupying only one room.[62] Other divided houses were large; in 1609 one in St. Mary's parish, probably in Headgate, comprised three low rooms or chambers, one of them a shop on the

47 Ibid. D/B 5 Cr109, rot. 13; D/Y 2/2, p. 13.
48 B.L. Stowe MS. 829, ff. 19v., 20v.–22.
49 P.R.O., E 178/819.
50 Ibid. STAC 2/23, no. 122; STAC 2/24, no. 225.
51 E.R.O., D/B 5 Cr109, rot. 8; Cr110, rot. 13 and d.; D/B 5 R1, f. 127.
52 Ibid. Acc. C338; ibid. D/B 5 Cr112, rott. 6d., 15d.
53 B.L. Stowe MS. 829, f. 16 and v.

54 Above, this chapter, Econ. (Readjustment and Recovery).
55 E.R.O., D/B 5 Gb1, 17 Mar. 1578.
56 Ibid. D/B 5 Cr142, rott. 10, 29d.; Cr157, rot. 7.
57 Ibid. D/B 5 Gb2, f. 95.
58 Ibid. ff. 70v., 78v.; D/B 5 Gb3, f. 28v.
59 Ibid. D/B 5 Cb1/6, f. 221. 60 Ibid. Acc. C47, CPL 311–18.
61 Ibid. D/B 5 Cr120, rot. 13; Cr158, rot. 19.
62 Ibid. D/B 5 Cb1/5, ff. 118, 342; Cb1/7, ff. 122, 171.

street frontage, the kitchen, buttery, bakehouse, and storehouse on the ground floor, with seven chambers on the first floor.[63]

There were no clearly-defined industrial or craft areas in the town, but most mariners, not surprisingly, lived at the Hythe. So did many merchants, 10 out of the 13 whose addresses were recorded between 1500 and 1619. Clothmakers tended to live and work to the east, north, and south of the walls, where water was readily available; about two thirds of the known clothiers and baymakers between 1500 and 1619 lived in St. Peter's or St. James's parish.[64] The clothmaker Nicholas Maynard had water piped to his East Street house and workshops from the Colne at East mill in 1549. By 1571 a tenter yard and a tenter garden adjoined the house and workshops, which seem to have survived as a large group of buildings at the bottom of East Hill in 1748.[65] In 1535 and 1545 the clothier Henry Webb had permission to bring water, presumably from Chiswell, to his house in North Street,[66] probably the early 16th-century building later the Marquis of Granby inn. A beam in its east wing bears a shield with the initials HW.[67] A clothier's house beyond North bridge included a 'folding shop' and a tenter yard in 1604, and there were other tenters in a field in North Street in 1606. Other clothworkers lived near Losebrook, outside South or St. Botolph's gate, in 1511 and 1525.[68] Many butchers lived in East and West Stockwell Streets, near the shambles, and as late as 1580 had slaughter-houses there.[69]

The few borough buildings were in the western half of High Street. The moot hall, near the corner with West Stockwell Street, apparently remained substantially unchanged from 1373–4 until its demolition in 1843. At the west end of the street was the corn market, stalls or galleries erected against the building known as St. Peter's 'rents' in 1546, the Red Row by 1549. The 'rents' were apparently rebuilt by the prior of the Crutched friars before 1517. They were sold before the Dissolution, and passed through several hands before being acquired by the borough.[70] The borough repaired or rebuilt the corn market between 1627 and 1629, and by 1631 the rooms above the Red Row formed the Dutch Bay Hall.[71] West of St. Runwald's church, a market cross with an open ground floor and a room above replaced the medieval butter market or stall c. 1590. The town butchers' shambles, which stood in the middle of the street east of St. Runwald's, were rebuilt in 1583–4 as a substantial, two-storeyed structure. The fish market, in front of the Red Lion inn and its adjoining houses, was held in privately owned stalls.[72] When in 1557 the clerk of the market was appointed to oversee the maintenance and repair of buildings belonging to the town, only the bridges and mills were specifically mentioned; even the moot hall was included among 'other buildings'.[73] The borough repaired the 'ruinous' North and East bridges in 1631. Little attempt was made to maintain the town walls, or even, apparently, the gates.[74]

The castle, which had dominated the medieval town, was allowed to fall into decay in the 15th and 16th centuries. The bailey buildings fell down, and by 1622 much of the bailey wall had also gone, and houses were encroaching onto the site

[63] Ibid. D/B 5 Cb1/8, ff. 72v.–73; D/B 5 Gb2, f. 180 and v.
[64] Goose, 'Econ. and Social Aspects', 222–3.
[65] E.R.O., D/B 5 Cr117, rot. 7; Cr136, rot. 4 and d.; Morant, Colch. map facing p. 4.
[66] B.L. Stowe MS. 834, f. 82 and v.; E.R.O., D/B 5 Cr116, rot. 12 and d.
[67] E.R. xxxiii. 103–5; R.C.H.M. Essex, iii. 61.
[68] E.R.O., D/B 5 Cb1/5, f. 385; Cb1/8, ff. 72v.–73;

D/B 5 Cr84, rot. 6; Cr95, rot. 10d.
[69] Ibid. D/B 5 Cr142, rot. 10.
[70] Ibid. D/B 5 Cr115, rot. 8; Cr135, rot. 3d.; B.L. Stowe MS. 829, f. 31; Morant, Colch. 111.
[71] E.R.O., D/B 5 Gb3, f. 103v.; below, Markets.
[72] E.R.O., D/B 5 Cr87, rot. 18; below, Markets.
[73] E.R.O., D/B 5 Cr123, rot. 10.
[74] Below, Communications (Bridges); Walls etc.

of its ditch. St. Giles's church was remodelled, and given a south porch and a new north chapel in the early 16th century. The tower of All Saints' church was rebuilt *c*. 1500, that of St. Mary's-at-the-Walls *c*. 1534, and north vestries were added to St. Leonard's and St. Peter's about the same time,[75] but no work seems to have been done after the Reformation. The tall, 'stately contrived' water house and works in Windmill field west of the town were built in 1620 by alderman Thomas Thurston.[76]

The Civil War and Siege

At the start of the Civil War in 1642 the town defences were improved, ramparts being built behind lost or weakened sections of the wall. By 1643 'forts', perhaps including an outwork on the north-east corner of the walls, had been added. The siege of 1648 caused extensive destruction, particularly in the suburbs, which were burnt by both sides to deprive the enemy of cover and to open up lines of fire. Sir John Lucas's house at St. John's Abbey, Sir Harbottle Grimston's at the Crutched Friars, and Henry Barrington's in the fields south-east of the town were among those destroyed.[77]

Eyewitnesses at the end of the siege described 'many fair houses' and 'fair streets … of stately houses' burnt to ashes.[78] In March 1649 at least 193 tax-paying houses were still derelict having been burnt or pulled down during the siege: 53 in St. Botolph's, 51 in St. Mary's-at-the-Walls, 35 in St. James's (including the rectory house), 32 in Holy Trinity, 17 in St. Giles's, and 5 in St. Martin's.[79] Many poorer houses and cottages, particularly in St. Mary Magdalen's, were also destroyed. A tax assessment made in July 1649 confirms that the worst damage was in St. Botolph's, St. Giles's, and St. Mary's-at-the-Walls parishes, which were each granted a reduction of over a third in their tax. St. Peter's, St. James's, St. Leonard's, and St. Runwald's were each granted a reduction of between a quarter and a third, while the assessments of the remaining intramural parishes were reduced by between 15 and 24 per cent.[80]

Most private houses were quickly rebuilt or repaired; several were already under repair in December 1648.[81] The borough granted building leases of two plots of land 'in', presumably by, the postern, perhaps the sites of houses near St. Mary's-at-the-Walls destroyed in the siege, in 1651. Elsewhere, the sites of three burnt houses in St. Botolph's Street, by the priory entrance, were still tofts or parcels of ground in 1654.[82] The suburbs were said to be under repair in 1656, but sites in Crouch Street and Priory Street were still vacant then and in 1659.[83] The site of two burnt houses at the north end of North bridge seems to have remained empty for several years, although new houses had been built by 1683.[84] As late as 1698 Magdalen Street apparently still bore marks of the siege.[85] Henry Barrington's house had been rebuilt by 1656, but the Lucas house at St. John's and Sir Harbottle Grimston's Crutched Friars never recovered from the siege.[86] Three churches were 'ruined': St. Botolph's, St. Giles's, and St. Mary's-at-the-Walls; St. Martin's and St. Mary Magdalen's were 'decayed' in 1650, presumably

75 Below, Castle; Churches.
76 *East Anglian N. & Q.* N.S. iii. 31; below, Public Services.　　　77 Above, Fig. 8.
78 J. Rushworth, *Hist. Colln.* vii. 1242; *True Relation of the Taking of Colch.* (1648): copy in E.C.L. Colch.
79 E.R.O., D/Y 2/2, p. 304; ibid. T/A 465/106 (Boro. Mun., Acc. C1, assessment of 1649); Smith, *Eccl. Hist. Essex*, 318–19.

80 B.L. Stowe MS. 833, f. 64.
81 E.R.O., D/B 5 Gb4, f. 24v.
82 Ibid. f. 55; D/DMb T55.
83 Ibid. D/DC 22/27; D/DO T955; *Diary of John Evelyn*, ed. E. S. de Beer, iii. 176–7.
84 E.R.O., Boro. Mun., Ct. R. 200, rot. 8.
85 *Journeys of Celia Fiennes*, ed. C. Morris, 142–3.
86 E.R.O., D/Q 30/1/4, no. 2; below, Religious Houses.

as a result of the fighting.[87] All five churches remained unrepaired throughout the later 17th century; St. Runwald's was also out of repair for much of the century, and St. Nicholas's was extensively damaged by the fall of its tower *c.* 1700. Their ruins gave an aura of decay to the otherwise rebuilt town. Daniel Defoe in 1722 reported that the town 'still mourns in the ruins of a civil war' and referred to its 'battered walls, breaches in the turrets, and ruined churches'.[88]

The Later 17th Century

The built-up area continued to expand, particularly in Moor Elms Lane (Priory Street) where houses were being built on the waste in 1658 and before 1672, and another house had been divided into four by 1683.[89] Building leases were granted in 1681 for land at Knaves Acre in the Hythe and for a two-storeyed house with two rooms on each floor, 'well tiled, glazed, and finished', in the postern in St.

FIG. 9. PART OF A PROSPECT OF COLCHESTER FROM THE NORTH, 1697
showing the tower of St. Peter's church on the left, the roofless tower of St. Mary's on the right
with the windmill beside it, and tenter grounds in the foreground to the right

Peter's parish.[90] A house built after the siege on the site of Botolph's barn outside South gate had been divided by 1683.[91] In the central area, division of large houses continued: ten rooms, including the hall, shop, and kitchen, with four chambers above them, had been separated from the rest of the former King's Arms or Sun inn in High Street by 1682. A messuage sold in 1684 was clearly composed of rooms once part of one or two houses; it comprised the passage from the street to the yard, the low room next to the street with the chamber over it, a chamber over part of an adjoining building, a staircase leading to the two chambers, a shop, and a back buttery.[92] Other divided houses were recorded regularly in the 1680s and 1690s.[93] When a house in St. James's parish was divided in 1706, one occupant

[87] Smith, *Eccl. Hist. Essex*, 318–19.
[88] Daniel Defoe, *Tour*, ed. G. D. H. Cole (1927), i. 16.
[89] E.R.O., D/B 5 Gb4, f. 173; Gb5, f. 72; ibid. Boro. Mun., Ct. R. 200, rot. 4d.
[90] Ibid. D/B 5 Gb5, ff. 180, 182.
[91] Ibid. Boro. Mun., Ct. R. 200, rot. 11.
[92] Ibid. Ct. R. 201, rot. 11.
[93] Ibid. Ct. R. 200, rot. 1; 201, rott. 4, 12; 202, rot. 9; 207, rot. 1d.; 208, rot. 1; 216, rot. 5.

1   Hythe Hill and East Hill, showing on the left St. Leonard's church at the Hythe

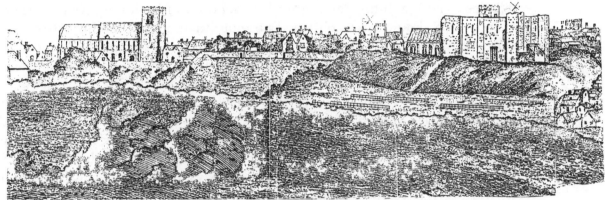

2.   The eastern end of the walled town, showing on the left St. James's church, and on the right the castle and its earthworks with, to the left and behind it, the nave and tower of All Saints' church; in the foreground are tenter grounds for drying cloth

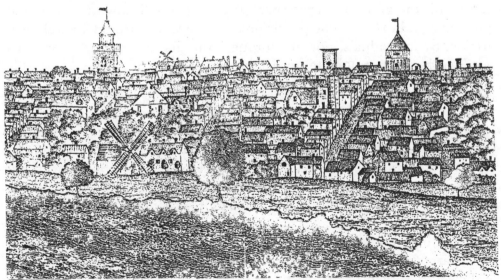

3   The centre of the town: on the left is the tower of St. Nicholas's church (which collapsed c. 1700, largely destroying the medieval church); in front and to the right of St. Nicholas's is the large Presbyterian meeting-house; on the skyline at the right are the towers of St. Runwald's (demolished in 1878) and Holy Trinity churches

COLCHESTER FROM THE NORTH, 1697

further details of Maheux's Prospect

was required to build a new brick wall between the two portions.[94] By then demand for houses had eased. A 'newly built' house near North bridge was empty in 1708, and a house outside the walls in St. Mary's-at-the-Walls parish which fell down between 1673 and 1709 was not rebuilt.[95]

The market place was reorganized in 1659 and 1660, the fish market being moved from High Street to St. Nicholas's Street, and the country butchers' stalls demolished. The town butchers' shambles remained east of St. Runwald's church, but fewer butchers seem to have lived in East and West Stockwell Streets than in the 16th century and the early 17th.[96] The earlier concentrations of clothworkers near the river declined in the 17th century, but by the end of the century there was a large group of possibly industrial buildings in Ostrich Yard outside Ryegate besides that at the bottom of East Hill.[97] Fewer merchants were recorded in St. Leonard's at the Hythe, only 7 out of the 20 known to have lived in the town between 1619 and 1700, and the relative wealth of that parish declined.[98] Nevertheless in 1692 John Barrington was accused of building a warehouse on land there which should have contained no more than a fence, and by 1689 there was a 'new building' and a coalyard beside Hythe mill.[99] Improvements made to the navigation of the Colne under an Act of 1698,[1] presumably encouraged further commercial development in the early 18th century.

Despite the relative prosperity of the later 17th-century town, little public building was done. Indeed, the top storey of the castle was blown off with gunpowder in the 1690s and the reorganization of the market place seems to have involved more demolition than building.[2] The Red Row or Bay Hall was still in 1698 'a long building like stalls' on which the bays were exposed for sale. The streets, however, were then broad and well pitched.[3] The borough maintained North, East, and Hythe bridges, using stone from the partially demolished castle in 1696 and 1698, and borrowing £350 for the repair of the bridges, moot hall, and part of High Street in 1701. The town wall between Head gate and Scheregate was level with the ground *c.* 1700; part of East gate fell down in 1652, and more was pulled down in 1676.[4] The provision of piped water, from Chiswell, was again undertaken by individuals, not the borough; the first attempt in 1687 failed, and the waterworks did not operate until 1707.[5]

The Buildings

Most houses were timber-framed and plastered, with tiled roofs. Except in High Street and at the top of North Hill where there were three-storeyed houses, they were of two storeys with attics. Celia Fiennes observed in 1698 that 'the fashion of the country lies much in long roofs and great cantilevers and peaks'.[6] As the single-storeyed halls were rebuilt to provide more accommodation, especially when they were on the street frontage, so jettied construction, which had been usual on cross wings, became common along the whole length of frontages. The jettied northern part of no. 30 East Stockwell Street occupies the site of the medieval hall, while the southern half of the west side of Trinity Street appears to be a uniform range of jettied buildings of the 16th century. The fashion for jettying continued

94 Ibid. Ct. R. 224, rot. 2d.
95 Ibid. Ct. R. 225, rot. 6; 226, rot. 10.
96 Goose, 'Econ. and Social Aspects', 222; below, Markets.
97 Morant, *Colch.* map facing p. 4; E.R.O., Boro. Mun., Ct. R. 226, rot. 9.
98 Goose, 'Econ. and Social Aspects', 222.
99 E.R.O., D/B 5 Gb5, ff. 351, 354; ibid. Boro. Mun., Ct.

R. 208, rot. 1.
1 Below, Port.
2 Below, Castle; Markets.
3 *Journeys of Celia Fiennes*, 142–3.
4 E.R.O., D/B 5 Gb6, p. 233; below, Communications (Bridges); Castle; Walls.   5 Below, Public Services (Water Supply).
6 *Journeys of Celia Fiennes*, 143.

into the later 17th century, the latest certain example being nos. 83–84 High Street, dated 1680. Whereas the early brackets were thin and had a simple curve, the later ones were broad and often incorporated a scroll. With the fashion for long jetties and heavy brackets went one for large gables rising off the eaves. Structurally the gables are secondary to the main ridge, which is normally parallel to the street, and they are sometimes jettied like the floor below. Nos. 29–32 West Stockwell Street has jetties and large gables on a house whose three-roomed plan with a large internal stack is of a characteristically rural type.

Houses varied in size from the large town houses of the duke of Norfolk and Thomas Audley, which became the Red Lion and the King's Head inns respectively, to merchants' houses with warehouses round a courtyard, like Winsleys at the eastern end of High Street, and to two-roomed cottages or 'rents'.[7] Headgate House, the former King's Head inn, is arranged around the east, north, and west sides of a courtyard off the west side of Head Street. The tall west range has walls of brick which incorporate at the south end a doorway with four-centred head and a large first-floor fireplace of similar form, perhaps part of Audley's house or that of his successor Richard Duke, clerk of the court of Augmentations.[8] A range was added to the back in the earlier 18th century to form an assembly room for the inn. The north range is timber-framed, and probably 17th-century; the east range, which incorporates the carriageway to the street, is also timber-framed. Tymperleys off Trinity Street, claimed as the house of William Gilberd (d. 1603), incorporates the 15th-century timber-framed parlour range of a house of which the hall was probably immediately to the east and parallel to the street. The range preserved in the house to the south was probably adjacent to the service end of the hall. The hall was demolished in the 16th or 17th century, and a linking range built between the parlour and the street range of the house. The parlour range was extended westwards on more than one occasion.

Tile was used for roofs of quite modest houses by the mid 16th century,[9] and brick was used in grand houses such as the former King's Head inn and for chimneys early in the century. A borough lease of 1617 required a new house to have a tiled roof and a brick chimney, and similar leases of 1619 and 1629 prohibited the use of thatch.[10] The borough was erecting a brick building in 1618, and an L-shaped brick house of c. 1620 survived in Northgate Street in the early 20th century. Brick warehouses were built at the Hythe in 1623.[11] Nevertheless brick houses were still sufficiently unusual in the 1680s for one outside Scheregate and one in St. Mary's-at-the-Walls to be so named, and brick-built houses were so described in 1702 and 1703.[12] Before 1698 wealthy Quakers, perhaps members of the Furley family in Holy Trinity parish, had built a few brick houses 'in the London mode'.[13] The houses may have been only brick fronted, and may indeed have been those at the north end of Trinity Street whose mid 17th-century façade of orange brick decorated with a plinth and pilasters survived, encased in a later building, in the 1980s.[14] Such refronting became more general later in the century.[15] Encroachment in front of houses in Holy Trinity parish in 1696 and in All Saints' in 1697 may have been infillings under overhanging first floors. So may that of the

7 Colch. Arch. Group, *Bull.* xxxi. 9–12; E.R.O., Boro. Mun., Ct. R. 215, rot. 4.
8 E.R.O., D/B 5 Cr114, rot. 8; Cr115, rot. 8.
9 e.g. P.R.O., STAC 2/23/122.
10 E.R.O., D/B 5 Gb2, ff. 160v., 180 and v.; Gb3, f. 88.
11 Ibid. D/B 5 Gb2, f. 165v.; Gb3, f. 28v.; R.C.H.M.

Essex, 62.
12 E.R.O., Boro. Mun., Ct. R. 202, rot. 3; 209, rot. 4; 219, rot. 12; 220, rot. 8.
13 *Journeys of Celia Fiennes*, 142–3.
14 *Colch. Arch. Rep.* vi. 347–54.
15 R.C.H.M. *Essex*, iii. 54.

HEADGATE COURT, 1993
formerly the King's Head Inn

THE 'SIEGE HOUSE', c. 1910

owner of the house next to the Red Lion, who in 1703 was encroaching on the road to enlarge his shop.[16]

Most houses in the main streets had shops on at least part of their street frontage, often with a parlour or hall on the street or immediately behind it. Other buildings, including warehouses, were grouped round courtyards entered by a great gate.[17] In the later 17th century the plaster of outer walls, particularly on gables, was often decorated with pargetting, described by a French visitor in 1698 as 'all raised into ornaments stamped upon the plaster, as we impress a seal upon wax; heads of beasts, festoons, cartridges, animals, and compartments, etc. all wretchedly designed and worse executed.' An early surviving example on the gable of no. 37 North Hill is dated 1666.[18] By the late 16th century merchants had glass in their windows and wainscot in their halls and parlours.[19] Re-used heraldic glass in the Siege House in East Street in 1922, apparently from another Colchester house, contained the date 1546 and the initials WS, perhaps for William Strachey, merchant, bailiff in 1555.[20] A clothier's house beyond East bridge in 1630 had a wainscoted hall with a parlour opening off it and another room opening off the parlour. A saymaker's house in St. Botolph's parish also had wainscoting and glass windows in 1638.[21] An elaborate, early 17th-century plaster ceiling survived in a house in Maidenburgh Street in 1922.[22]

Many inns stood near the town gates, like the Maidenhead on the corner of Crouch Street and Maldon Road, recorded from 1554 until its licence was revoked for disorders in 1698.[23] Others like the Crown, where plays were performed in 1566, were at the Hythe,[24] but the main inns, like other large houses, were concentrated in Head Street, North Hill, and High Street.

The Bell, the Crown, and the New inn or the White (later the Red) Lion, stood side by side on the south side of High Street in 1522.[25] The White Lion had been built as a town house for John Howard, Lord Howard, later duke of Norfolk, in 1481 or 1482, and seems to have become an inn between 1501 and 1515 when it was the New inn, with a sign on the street.[26] It was one of three inns appointed as wine taverns in 1604.[27] The Bell and the Crown were private houses by 1597.[28] The George, presumably the surviving inn on the north side of High Street, was recorded in 1551 and 1566.[29] In 1617 a total of 331 free burgesses ate an election dinner there in the gatehouse chamber, the rose chamber, the cock chamber, the George chamber, the lower parlour, the kitchen chamber, the street parlour, the hall, and the cellar.[30] The White Hart on the south side of High Street in St. Peter's parish, another of the licensed wine taverns of 1604, was an inn in 1539 and was still one in 1705. It accommodated 156 people for an election dinner in 1579.[31] The Angel, the third licensed wine tavern in 1604, was an L-shaped building on the corner of High Street and West Stockwell Street, probably with a hall parallel to High Street. First recorded by that name in 1517, it was an inn or at least an alehouse in 1585.[32]

[16] E.R.O., D/B 5 Gb6, pp. 70, 106, 280.
[17] e.g. E.R.O., D/B 5 Cb1/6, f. 221; Colch. Arch. Group, Bull. xxxi. 9–10, 27.
[18] M.[Henri de Valbourg] Misson's Memoirs and Observations in his Travels over Eng. (1719), 40; Colch. Arch. Group, Bull. xxix. 16–17.
[19] E.R.O., D/B 5 Cr154, rot. 5d.; Cr158, rot. 14d.; Cr162, rot. 9d.
[20] R.C.H.M. Essex, iii. 70; E.R.O., D/B 5 R1, f. 133.
[21] E.R.O., D/B 5 Cb1/9, f. 68v.; Cb1/10, f. 483v.
[22] R.C.H.M. Essex, iii. 63.
[23] E.R.O., D/B 5 Sb2/2, ff. 1–20v.; D/B 5 Cr120, rot. 14d.; D/B 5 Cb1/8, ff. 282v.–283; D/B 5 Sb4/2, 11 Aug. 1698; D/DU 289/13; Emmison, Elizabethan Life: Disorder, 215.

[24] Ibid. D/B 5 R5, f. 79v.; D/B 5 Cr153, rot. 20d.
[25] Ibid. D/B 5 Cr93, rot. 13.
[26] J. Harvey, Eng. Med. Architects (1984), 302; B.L. Add. Ch. 215; Bodl. MS. Rolls Essex 2.
[27] E.R.O., D/B 5 Gb2, f. 40.
[28] Ibid. D/B 5 Cr158, rot. 19.
[29] Ibid. D/B 5 Cr119, rot. 6; D/B 5 R5, ff. 76v.–77.
[30] Ibid. D/B 5 Ab1/8, rot. 19.
[31] Ibid. D/B 5 Ab1/2; D/B 5 Gb2, f. 40; D/B 5 Cr109, rot. 4d.; D/B 5 Sr76, rot. 7; ibid. Acc. C210, J. B. Harvey Colln. v, p. 51.
[32] E.R.O., D/B 5 Gb2, f. 40; D/B 5 R2, f. 105v.; D/ACA 14, f. 104v.; Colch. Arch. Group, Bull. xxxi. 27–9.

The King's Head, in Head Street near Head gate, was an inn in the 1550s, and in 1565 its innholder was licensed to keep a 'tennis play' as recreation for gentlemen and 'other fit persons'.[33] As many as 232 freemen ate an election dinner there in 1600, occupying 'Mr. bailiffs chamber', the little building, the lower great building, the other lower building, the street parlour, the roof parlour, Michelle's chamber, and the hall.[34] The inn was probably the house in St. Mary's parish assessed on 22 hearths in 1671, the greatest number of hearths in any house in the town.[35]

BOROUGH GOVERNMENT

COLCHESTER'S judicial liberties were established by its medieval charters, confirmed by *inspeximus* in 1488, 1547, 1553, 1559, 1605, and 1629. To earlier privileges was added exemption from service as sheriff or escheator and from the jurisdiction of the county coroner, given by the charter of 1535 granting Kingswood heath to the borough.[36] In the late 16th century, however, the town lost its immunity from purveyance. The bailiffs acquiesced in a demand for fish in 1587 although some townsmen resisted the purveyor, but when in 1593 the town was assessed at £12 a year composition for purveyance, the corporation determined not to pay. In the ensuing dispute the purveyor seized cattle from the town's commons.[37] The town seems to have accepted defeat by 1597 when the bailiffs unsuccessfully petitioned Sir Robert Cecil for a reduction in their assessment.[38] The dissolution of St. John's abbey and St. Botolph's priory removed two rival liberties within the borough, but the claims of St. John's to exemption from the borough's jurisdiction were inherited by the Audleys and the Lucases. In 1565 Thomas Audley of Berechurch tried to exclude borough officials from his manor.[39] His widow Catherine refused to muster with the borough in 1580, and the following year she and Francis Jobson of Monkwick had themselves assessed for subsidy in Lexden hundred instead of in Colchester. An attempt by the borough sub-collectors to distrain on cattle in Berechurch in 1581 led to a riot.[40] In 1582 and 1583 the borough was in dispute with Sir Thomas Lucas, owner of St. John's abbey, over waste ground in Greenstead and other matters.[41]

Extensive privileges were granted to the Dutch congregation established in 1570 or 1571.[42] The Dutch were allowed their own church, although they had to pay church rates in the parishes in which they lived, and were responsible for the maintenance of their own poor. Most important, they controlled the trade in bays and says, which they were allowed to carry on without becoming freemen of the town. The two governors of the Dutch Bay Hall and their 22 assistants made and changed regulations for the bay trade, and their officers inspected and sealed all bays made in Colchester whether by Dutchmen or, increasingly in the 17th century, by Englishmen.[43] Although the Dutch contributed to subsidies and other taxes laid on the town, and were subject to the borough courts, their economic privileges placed them apart from the English and led to friction, particularly in the early

[33] *E.A.T.* 3rd ser. xv. 92; *Cal. Pat.* 1563–6, p. 329.

[34] E.R.O., D/B 5 Ab1/4.

[35] Ibid. Q/STh5; P.R.O., PROB 11/336, f. 143v.

[36] *Colch. Charters*, 56–9, 76–80.

[37] E.R.O., D/Y 2/6, pp. 17, 21, 23; D/B 5 Gb1, 29 Mar. 1593; 14 Mar. 1594; 2 Sept., 10 Nov. 1595; B.L. Lansdowne MS. 73, f. 118.

[38] *Cal. S.P. Dom.* 1595–7, 162; Hist. MSS. Com. 9, *Salisbury*, vii, p. 332; ix, p. 396.

[39] E.R.O., D/B 5 R5, f. 66v.

[40] Ibid. D/B 5 Ab1/2; D/B 5 Gb1, 30 May, 8 Nov. 1581; D/B 5 Sb2/4, ff. 4v.–5v.; D/DRg 1/117; *Acts of P.C.* 1581–2, 124.

[41] E.R.O., D/B 5 Gb1, 13 July 1582; 27 Aug. 1583; D/Y 2/7, p. 205.

[42] *Immigrants and Minorities*, i. 266–70.

[43] *V.C.H. Essex*, ii. 388; *Reg. Baptisms in Dutch Ch. at Colch.* (Huguenot Soc. xii), pp. i–xxvii, xli.

THE RED LION INN, 1993

NORTH HILL, 1951
east side, with the Marquis of Granby Inn and the tower of St. Peter's

17th century, when they were supported by the Privy Council.[44] The governors of the Dutch Bay Hall retained their control of the bay trade until 1728.[45]

The composition of the freeman body, Colchester's governing class, became a matter of increasing concern to the borough officers in the 16th and 17th centuries. The medieval practice whereby all men born in the borough were entitled to enter the freedom without fee survived until *c.* 1550 when that right was apparently restricted to the sons of freemen.[46] In 1565 all those claiming the freedom by birth were ordered to be sworn in the borough court at the age of 20, paying no more than 2*d.* to the clerk and 4*d.* to the serjeants. Non-resident freemen were ordered to come to elections.[47] An order of 1523, repeated *c.* 1550 and in 1583, allowed the admission of a freeman's former apprentice for a fine of 3*s.* 4*d.*, provided that the apprenticeship of seven or more years had been registered at its start, and the order for such registration was repeated in 1660.[48] In 1637 the fine for the admission of 'foreigners' was raised to £10, and they were required to be approved by representatives of their craft; in 1654 the consent of the borough assembly was required.[49]

The number of active freemen fluctuated, but seems to have increased overall in the earlier 17th century, from perhaps *c.* 450 in 1619 to *c.* 900 in 1646. Numbers seem to have fallen in the later 17th century, but rose rapidly at its end, perhaps reaching *c.* 1,100 in 1704.[50] In the early 18th century freedoms were sold to raise money, and the system was also blatantly manipulated for political purposes: 234 men were admitted by birth or apprenticeship in 1700–1, and 39 bought their freedom from Ralph Creffield, mayor 1702–3. In 1705 the practice of admitting large numbers of men either by purchase or on dubious grounds was said to be 'an invasion of the rights and privileges of the honest free burgesses', but the sale of freedoms was complained of again in 1711 and 1713.[51]

Officers and Politics 1485–1635

Until 1635 Colchester was governed under the provisions of the charter of 1462. The principal officers were the 2 bailiffs who with the 8 other aldermen, 16 members of the first council, and 16 members of the second council, formed the common council of the borough, known by the 16th century as the assembly. The bailiffs and 2 aldermen, with the recorder, were J.P.s; 2 aldermen served as coroners, and 2 aldermen and 2 councillors as keykeepers, responsible for the common chest in which the borough seal, plate, records, and money were kept.[52] Those officers, with the chamberlain who was responsible for the borough's day to day finances, were elected annually. In the early 16th century the method and dates of election were those laid down in 1372. At a meeting of the borough court early in September the free burgesses elected 4 headmen, 1 from among the wealthier burgesses in each of the 4 wards, and each headman chose 5 other substantial burgesses from his ward, making a total of 24, who elected the officers. At the end of September another college of 24, similarly chosen, elected the town clerk and 4 serjeants at mace.[53] Despite the annual elections, by the 15th century aldermen and councillors normally held office for life, or until ill health or removal

44 E.R.O., D/B 5 Cb1/6, ff. 93, 440; B.L. Lansdowne MS. 157, ff. 101–102v.
45 Below, Georgian Colch. (Econ., Decline of Bay Trade).
46 E.R.O., D/B 5 R2, f. 231v.
47 Ibid. D/B 5 R5, ff. 107v.–108.
48 Ibid. D/B 5 R2, ff. 31, 232; D/B 5 Gb1, 27 Aug. 1583; Gb4, f. 230.
49 Ibid. D/B 5 Gb3, f. 172; Gb4, f. 125.
50 Ibid. D/B 5 Aa1/1–26: number of election dinners paid for.
51 Ibid. Boro. Mun., 'Colch. MSS.' 1620–1770, ff. 4 and v., 19v.–28; D/B 5 Sr75, rot. 5; D/B 5 Gb6, pp. 423–4; Gb7, f. 13.
52 Colch. Charters, 40–54; E.R.O., D/B 5 Gb2, f. 147v.
53 E.R.O., D/Y 2/2, pp. 17–20.

from the borough caused them to resign. When a vacancy occurred, new aldermen were chosen from among the first councillors.

The path to civic office started with the second council, although a few wealthy men went straight into the first council, from which their promotion was usually rapid. Of the *c*. 200 men known to have entered the first council in the 16th century, 79 became aldermen and 2 refused that office; a high proportion of the others served only a few years as councillors. There was only a small group of men like Winkin Greenrice, a Fleming, who were councillors for many years and served as keykeepers without becoming aldermen. Service as, or refusal to serve as, chamberlain seems to have been irrelevant to a man's later career in the 16th century: 34 of the 79 aldermen are known to have served as chamberlain and 11 refused, compared with the 39 chamberlains and 18 refusers who rose no higher than the first council. In the 17th century, however, service as chamberlain was more important. Only six of the 16th-century aldermen failed to reach the rank of bailiff, and that failure was probably due to premature death or retirement; only one of them, William Thompson (alderman 1594–7) served for as many as four years.

In 1591 it was claimed that by 'ancient order' aldermen should serve as bailiff only every four or five years, and on average they did so throughout the 16th century. Those who, like John Christmas between 1516 and 1547, Benjamin Clere between 1541 and 1575, and John Best between 1547 and 1571, served seven or eight terms as bailiff, did so because of their long tenure of office as alderman, 32, 35, and 26 years respectively. There is no evidence for a ruling clique within the ranks of the aldermen.[54] Most bailiffs were clothiers or merchants; one of the few who was not, Henry Osborne, was abused in 1610 as a man who lived by cutting leather and selling gloves, and a fool whose name had been 'in question for light behaviour'.[55]

Aldermen and councillors provided their own livery gowns, which were worn for council meetings and sermons and when the corporation officially visited the midsummer and St. Dennis's fairs. The aldermen wore scarlet gowns, the councillors purple until 1598 when they were ordered to provide themselves with black gowns faced with lambskin and with black and scarlet hoods, like the London livery gowns.[56]

Three incidents in the early 16th century led to attempts to strengthen the officers' position. In 1514 about 40 men, including a councillor, disrupted the annual elections.[57] In 1520 the retiring bailiff, William Debenham, refused to attend the swearing in of the new bailiffs or to serve as alderman, and the following year he, with others including the councillor Christopher Hammond, indicted two aldermen and the town clerk, Thomas Audley, at the county sessions at Chelmsford for attacking a house in Colchester.[58] Debenham took no further part in borough government, but Hammond became bailiff in 1525 and served as alderman until 1530.

Ordinances in 1523 confirmed the existing practice that no alderman could be removed from office at the annual election without the consent of a majority of the other aldermen. More detailed constitutions in 1524 repeated that ordinance, and abolished the second election day, providing that the bailiffs should appoint the

54   Ibid. D/Y 2/8, p. 157; Boro. Mun., Ct. R. Transcripts 1510–1600; J. R. Davis, 'Colch. 1600–62: Politics, Religion and Officeholding in an Eng. Provincial Town' (Brandeis Univ. Ph.D. thesis, 1980), 479–80.

55   E.R.O., D/B 5 Sb2/6, f. 200v.
56   *E.J.* xxiii. 65.
57   E.R.O., D/B 5 Cr86, rot. 5.
58   Ibid. D/B 5 Cr92, rot. 18d.; Cr93, rot. 3.

BOURNE MILL IN 1892
the house was built as a fishing lodge by Sir Thomas Lucas in 1591

TYMPERLEYS *c.* 1890
the house before the 20th-century alterations

serjeants at mace, and the bailiffs, aldermen and common council the town clerk.[59] In 1529 the 24 electors were given a voice in the appointment of serjeants, being allowed to choose four men from eight nominated to them by the bailiffs and aldermen.[60]

When disputes between the officers, councillors, and free burgesses reached parliament in 1549 commissioners, among them Francis Jobson, confirmed and defined the 'ancient and laudable' custom of the town. Only free burgesses who were householders and were not victuallers, attorneys in the courts, or 'loose journeymen' might vote for the headmen, who were to be worth 40s. a year in lands or £40 in goods; the 20 electors chosen by the headmen were to be similarly qualified. There were to be two election days. On the first, the Monday after the beheading of St. John the Baptist (29 Aug.), the 24 were to choose the aldermen, bailiffs, J.P.s, recorder, and chamberlain. On the second, the Tuesday after Michaelmas, a new electoral college of 24 was to chose the coroners, keykeepers, town clerk, and serjeants at mace. The 16 first councillors were to be chosen by the bailiffs and aldermen on the Monday after Michaelmas, and they with the bailiffs and aldermen were then to chose 16 others, 4 from each ward, to serve on the second council. The bailiffs, aldermen, and chamberlain were to be sworn in in the moot hall on Michaelmas day.[61]

There was an unusually high turnover of councillors in the decade 1550–9, and John Beriff and two other aldermen were removed at the elections in 1559. That year William Beriff, a clothier and servant of Sir Francis Jobson, was deprived of his freedom for attacking an alderman and libelling a councillor.[62] Richard Thurston's initial refusal in 1574 to serve as alderman, an office to which he had been elected after apparently retiring from the first council, seems to have led to a series of ordinances tightening the rules for the swearing in of officers and prescribing fines for those who tried to evade office or failed to carry out its duties.[63]

Serious disputes broke out between different factions in the town in 1575 and 1576.[64] The immediate cause was the excessive punishment for adultery meted out to the mariner John Lone, but the underlying one was opposition to Thomas Upcher, rector of St. Leonard's, and other Calvinist clergy, and to their supporters, alderman Benjamin Clere and the recorder Sir Thomas Lucas. Townsmen presumably remembered Clere's cruelty to protestant martyrs in Mary's reign, and he was also accused of enriching his family at the town's expense, notably in making his teenage son master of St. Mary Magdalen's hospital.[65] In the summer of 1575 a series of increasingly scurrilous libels, directed first at Upcher and his associates then at Clere, circulated in the town. At first they seem to have generated sympathy for Clere, and that autumn he and his friend Robert Mott were elected bailiffs. John Hunwick, apparently an opponent of Lucas and the only alderman who had opposed Lone's punishment,[66] was removed from office. Their pursuit of the libellers, however, appears soon to have swung public opinion against Clere and Lucas. In the winter of 1575–6 the dispute reached both the Privy Council and Star Chamber, and the collection of an aid to defray the town's expenses added to Clere's unpopularity; both he and Lucas were removed from office at the elections of 1576. The electors chose their opponent John Hunwick bailiff, but the Privy

59   Ibid. D/B 5 R2, ff. 30–32v. Other ordinances seem to have remained in force for only a year.
60   Ibid. f. 33.   61   Ibid. D/Y 2/2, pp. 17–20.
62   Ibid. D/B 5 Cr125, rott. 1–2d.
63   Ibid. D/B 5 R7, ff. 256v.–257v.

64   M. S. Byford, 'The Price of Protestantism: Assessing the Impact of Religious Change on Elizabethan Essex: the Cases of Heydon and Colch. 1558–1594' (Oxf. Univ. D.Phil. thesis, 1988), 194–258.   65   E.R.O., D/B 5 Sr2.
66   Acts of P.C. 1571–5, 41, 61.

Council declared the election void because Hunwick was not then an alderman.[67] In the course of the year 1576–7 Hunwick was restored to his place as alderman and was elected bailiff in 1577. The following year Clere and his son John were accused of campaigning for office,[68] but if they did so, they were unsuccessful. Despite further libels in March 1579, the corporation was able that autumn to assure Sir Francis Walsingham, the recorder, that the controversies were over, and that the last borough election had been 'so peaceable as to be soon finished'.[69]

Further troubles and dissension in the 1580s[70] led to new attempts to control elections. In 1585 it was agreed that there should be only one election day, the Monday after the beheading of St. John the Baptist. The following year the rules for the election of the first council by the bailiffs and aldermen and of the second council by the bailiffs, aldermen, and first councillors were re-issued.[71] In 1587 ordinances restricted the number of freemen entitled to vote by excluding those convicted of adultery, fornication, drunkenness, or swearing, besides victuallers and those who were not householders. Only one man from each ward was to nominate the headman, the others were to agree or if necessary to choose between two candidates by show of hands. The financial qualifications for headmen and electors were raised to land worth £4 a year although the value of goods needed to qualify remained at £40, and at least two of the five electors from each ward were to be members of the common council. The practice of having two election days was restored, but the second was to be for the serjeants at mace only.[72] In 1588 provision was made for a deputy town clerk, to be nominated and appointed by the corporation.[73]

In 1593 John Hunwick was again elected bailiff, although he had retired as an alderman in 1586. His election was declared void, but within two days he was elected a member of the first council, an alderman, and bailiff.[74] In 1595 the town was split on religious lines; the electors refused to proceed to an election and the bailiffs, aldermen, and common council elected the officers for the following year.[75] In 1603 a shoemaker, claiming that the headmen had not been properly chosen, tried to prevent the electors getting into the court room for the election. When it was held, Thomas Hazlewood was elected bailiff although he had been removed as alderman in 1596 and had only just been re-elected to the first council.[76]

Those and other disorders and 'tumultuous assemblies' reflect a dispute between the free burgesses and the officers which led to two attempts in 1612 to reform the method of election. The first, which would have increased the number of freemen eligible to vote, failed because the bailiffs, aldermen, and common council would not subscribe the new orders; the second, which would have reduced the number, because the free burgesses refused to accept the proposals. In 1615 the orders of 1587 were confirmed.[77] The same year a dispute over the removal of two aldermen and seven common councillors at the annual election reached King's Bench. In a comprehensive settlement, Sir Francis Bacon ordered that the officers, with a third alderman who had been removed in 1608, be restored to their places. He repeated the ordinance of 1523 forbidding the removal of aldermen without the consent of the rest of the bench, and extended the rule to common councillors, thus confirming

[67] E.R.O., D/Y 2/7, pp. 119–20.
[68] Ibid. D/B 5 Sb2/3, f. 123.
[69] *Acts of P.C.* 1578–80, 78; E.R.O., D/Y 2/9, pp. 257, 297; D/Y 2/7, p. 195.
[70] Byford, 'Price of Protestantism', 279.
[71] E.R.O., D/B 5 Gb1, 1 Nov. 1585; 20 Sept. 1586.
[72] Ibid. 11 Aug. 1587.   [73] Ibid. 14 Sept. 1588.

[74] Ibid. 17, 19 Sept. 1593.
[75] Ibid. 19 Sept. 1595; Hist. MSS. Com. 9, *Salisbury*, v, p. 394.
[76] E.R.O., D/B 5 Gb2 f. 37; D/B 5 Sb2/6, f. 85v.; Davis, 'Colch. 1600–62', 130.
[77] E.R.O., D/B 5 Gb2, ff. 109v.–112v., 115v.–118v.; Davis, 'Colch. 1600–62', pp. 131–3.

existing practice.[78] In 1624 one party in the corporation apparently wanted to exclude the free burgesses from borough elections, restricting the electorate to aldermen and councillors.[79]

A *quo warranto* brought against the borough charter between 1625 and 1631 was successfully resisted, and seems to have led to the confirmation of the borough's privileges by *inspeximus* in 1629, but further disputes resulted in a second challenge in 1633 and the resignation of the charter.[80] In 1635 a new charter reorganized borough government. The bailiffs were replaced by a mayor, the 16 first councillors were renamed assistants, and the 16 members of the second council common councillors. The mayor was to be chosen by the aldermen from two of their number nominated by those free burgesses entitled to vote under the 1587 ordinances. Aldermen, assistants, and common councillors were to hold office for life unless removed for bad behaviour by a majority of the officers and free burgesses; when a vacancy arose aldermen and councillors were to be chosen in the same way as the mayor, aldermen from among the assistants, common councillors from the free burgesses; assistants were to be chosen from among the councillors by a majority vote of the free burgesses. The recorder was to be elected by the officers, councillors, and free burgesses, and was to nominate the town or common clerk. The mayor was to have a casting vote in elections. He and the recorder might each appoint a deputy if they were unable to carry out their duties. The mayor, the recorder, the previous year's mayor, and two other aldermen were to be J.P.s. The officers to serve until the elections in 1636 were named in the charter, the aldermen, assistants, and common councillors being those elected in 1634.[81] Officers whose method of election was not specified in the charter (2 J.P.s, the coroners, keykeepers, and chamberlain) continued to be chosen by the electoral college. The assembly made special arrangements for the 1635 elections, which were not covered by the charter.[82] The charter gave the free burgesses a more direct say in the choice of mayor, aldermen, assistants, and councillors, but by finally abolishing annual elections except for the mayoralty it made more difficult the removal of serving officers.

The Civil War and Interregnum

By the 1640s there were divisions among the aldermen between those, headed by Robert Buxton, who had supported the king and Archbishop Laud, and those, led by Henry Barrington, who favoured parliament. The first mayoral election in 1647, of the royalist John Shaw, was annulled under pressure from a troop of parliamentarian horse, and the next man elected, John Cox, refused to serve.[83] After the siege of 1648 three aldermen (Robert Buxton, Thomas Laurence, and John Shaw), four assistants, and six common councillors who had supported, or were alleged to have supported, the royalists were removed, and the following year the moderate presbyterian recorder, Sir Harbottle Grimston, resigned.[84] Nevertheless two parties continued within the corporation, Henry Barrington's Cromwellian party being opposed by a more moderate group led by Thomas Reynolds. At the elections of 1654 Reynolds's party succeeded in removing Henry Barrington and his son Abraham, an assistant. Both sides petitioned Cromwell, who, after the 1655

78 E.R.O., D/Y 2/7, pp. 23–4, 241; D/B 5 Gb2, ff. 142v., 147v.
79 Ibid. D/B 5 Gb3, ff. 36, 38 and v.
80 *Cal. S.P. Dom.* 1633–4, 298, 313; P.R.O., PC 2/44, pp. 230–1. The first challenge was by Sir Robert Heath, attorney general 1625–31.
81 *Colch. Charters,* 81–103.
82 E.R.O., D/B 5 Gb3, ff. 141–2.
83 Ibid. D/B 5 Gb4, ff. 7v.–8; Hist. MSS. Com. 27, *12th Rep. IX, Beaufort,* 22–3; Davis, 'Colch. 1600–62', 337.
84 E.R.O., D/B 5 Gb4, ff. 22 and v., 31.

elections had returned a majority of the Reynolds party to office, sent Major-Gen. Hezekiah Haynes to Colchester to oversee new elections.[85] They were made in December 'with great difficulty': the removal of 'malignants' left only *c.* 100 free burgesses entitled to vote, only 74 of them 'honest', and the other party tried to elect John Shaw as recorder.[86] In 1656 a new charter abolished the 16 assistants and increased the number of councillors to 24, thus reducing the size of the corporation. It excluded the free burgesses from borough government, providing that all elections be made by the corporation alone.[87]

The Cromwellian charter was annulled in 1659. John Radhams, removed from the mayoralty in 1655, replaced Henry Barrington as mayor, and shortly afterwards Abraham Barrington and 3 other aldermen, 7 assistants, and the whole common council were removed or demoted.[88] In 1660 a further 4 aldermen, including John Furley the elder and Henry Barrington, 8 assistants, including the younger John Furley and Abraham Barrington, and 10 common councillors were replaced. John Shaw was restored to his place as alderman, and his son, another John Shaw, became recorder.[89] In 1661 an assistant and 3 common councillors, including the chamberlain, were removed.[90] The final purge of the corporation took place in 1662 under the Corporation Act. Four aldermen, including the mayor John Milbank and Jeremiah Daniell, 5 assistants, and 9 common councillors were removed.[91] Most of their replacements had little experience in borough government: Ralph Creffield, appointed alderman, was not even a common councillor.[92] A new charter of 1663 confirmed most of the provisions of the charter of 1635, but increased the number of aldermen from 10 to 12 (including the mayor), and the number of assistants and common councillors from 16 to 18 each. It also created the office of high steward.[93]

Borough Government and Politics 1663–1714

The controlling influence in the Restoration corporation seems to have been the younger John (later Sir John) Shaw, a supporter of the established church,[94] but opposition to his party grew during the 1670s. 'Scandalous' verses against Shaw and alderman William Moore circulated in 1673, and at the elections of 1676 the opposition, led by the aldermen Ralph Creffield, Nathaniel Laurence, and Thomas Green, all nonconformist sympathizers, succeeded in having Shaw removed as recorder. The resulting dispute lasted until the end of 1678, by which time Shaw was deputy to the new recorder, the duke of Albemarle.[95] In 1684 the 'loyal' aldermen John Rayner and William Boys accused Laurence, then mayor, Creffield, and Green of being covert dissenters, and 3 other aldermen and 15 assistants and councilmen of supporting them, enabling them to monopolize the office of mayor. The petition led to a threat of a *quo warranto* and to the surrender of the town's charter.[96]

The charter of 1684 reduced the number of assistants and common councillors to 15 each; it also excluded the free burgesses from elections which were to be

[85] Ibid. D/Y 2/7, p. 189; Bodl. MSS. Rawl. A 29, pp. 690, 692; Rawl. A 34, p. 125; Davis, 'Colch. 1600–62', 343–60.　　[86] Bodl. MS. Rawl. A 34, pp. 121, 129.

[87] *Cal. S.P. Dom.* 1655–6, 253, 371; 1656–7, 71, 79; Davis, 'Colch. 1600–62', 361; E.R.O., D/B 5 Gb4, f. 147v.

[88] E.R.O., D/B 5 Gb4, ff. 192v., 194v.–195; Davis, 'Colch. 1600–62', 60, 364–5.

[89] E.R.O., D/B 5 Gb4, ff. 208 and v., 225, 226v.; Davis, 'Colch. 1600–62', 365–6.

[90] E.R.O., D/B 5 Gb4, f. 362.

[91] Ibid. f. 363v.; Davis, 'Colch. 1600–62', 370.

[92] T. C. Glines, 'Politics and Government in the Borough of Colch. 1660–93' (Wisconsin Univ. Ph.D. thesis, 1974), 77.

[93] *Colch. Charters*, 104–26.

[94] Davis, 'Colch. 1600–62', 372–3.

[95] E.R.O., D/B 5 Sb2/9, ff. 205, 209v., 214; Glines, 'Politics and Govt. in Colch.' 142–9.

[96] Bodl. MS. Rawl. Essex 1, ff. 113–22, 126–31; Glines, 'Politics and Govt. in Colch.' 198–9.

made by the aldermen, assistants, and common councillors only. All officers were to be communicants of the Church of England and to subscribe the declaration under the Corporation Act, and all could be removed by the king or Privy Council at will. Nevertheless, the officers named in the charter were those elected in 1683; Creffield, Laurence, and Green remained aldermen, and John Stilman, accused of being 'factious' in 1684, continued as mayor.[97] Further attempts by the 'loyal party' to purge the dissenting party failed.[98] There was some difficulty in filling vacancies in the assembly in July 1687, but only one man, a common councillor, refused to take the oaths.[99]

In January and February 1688 the Privy Council ordered the replacement of the mayor, Alexander Hindmarsh, 6 aldermen, 10 assistants, 12 common councillors, the chamberlain, the high steward, and the recorder.[1] Those purged came from both parties in the borough and included aldermen Ralph Creffield and Nathaniel Laurence as well as the 'loyal' alderman William Moore. In May the high steward and recorder were again replaced, the recorder by Sir John Shaw. In September a new charter reduced the number of aldermen to 10 (including the mayor) and the numbers of assistants and common councillors to 10 each. The purges and the charter between them replaced the entire corporation except for two aldermen, Thomas Green, who had left the town in 1687, and John Rayner.[2]

By the end of August 1689 all the officers appointed in 1688 except John Rayner and 2 other aldermen, 3 assistants, and 2 common councillors had resigned, making borough government virtually impossible. Elections in which the free burgesses participated as they had before 1684 filled the vacancies in the offices created by the charter of 1688. Most of those elected, including all the aldermen, had served before 1684 and most had nonconformist sympathies, but Nathaniel Laurence, Ralph Creffield, and William Moore, the leaders of their respective factions, were not re-elected.[3] As negotiations for a new charter started, the 'nonconformist' party was accused, probably falsely, of trying to ensure that it excluded the free burgesses from elections.[4] The 1693 charter confirmed by *inspeximus* that of 1663; it also nullified the surrender of 1684 and all subsequent acts of the corporation, except demises of lands and farms.[5]

The two parties, by then aligned with the national Whig and Tory parties, dominated borough government in the late 17th century and the early 18th. At first the Tories seem to have had the upper hand. In 1695 alderman Samuel Mott, a former mayor and one of the dissenting faction in the 1680s, was removed from office and from his freedom after 'several allegations of misdemeanour'.[6] In 1696 Isaac Rebow, who was to become the leader of the Whig party, and seven other men, supported by Edmund Hickeringill, rector of All Saints', and by the aldermen Nathaniel Laurence the younger and John Seabrook, protested at the refusal of the senior alderman, William Moore, to proceed to the election of a new mayor to replace John Bacon, who had died in office.[7] Rebow was later accused of manipulating borough elections by treating free burgesses,[8] and in 1703, supported by the mayor Ralph Creffield the younger, he succeeded in defeating the Tory

97 *Colch. Charters*, 128–48; Glines, 'Politics and Govt. in Colch.' 201–5; B.L. Stowe MS. 835, f. 37.
98 Glines, 'Politics and Govt. in Colch.' 200–5.
99 E.R.O., D/B 5 Gb5, ff. 270, 272–274v.
1 Ibid. ff. 288, 290, 296v.–297; Glines, 'Politics and Govt. in Colch.' 227–37.
2 *Colch. Charters*, 149–69; E.R.O., D/B 5 Gb5, ff. 293, 294 and v., 297v., 298v.; Glines, 'Politics and Govt. in

Colch.' 229–36.
3 Glines, 'Politics and Govt. in Colch.' 256–9; E.R.O., D/B 5 Gb5, ff. 315–316v.
4 E.R.O., D/B 5 Gb6, p. 9; *Cal. S.P. Dom.* 1693, 296, 344.
5 *Colch. Charters*, 170–5; E.R.O., D/B 5 Gb5, ff. 360v., 361v.
6 E.R.O., D/B 5 Gb6, p. 36.
7 Ibid. Boro. Mun., 'Colch. MSS.' f. 7.
8 Bodl. MS. Rawl. C 441, f. 2.

candidate, Prince George of Denmark, for the office of high steward, although the prince's supporters alleged that he had at most 146 votes to the prince's 170.[9] There was trouble at the borough elections in 1713, and in 1714 Sir Isaac Rebow was rushed through the offices of councillor and assistant to that of alderman in two or three days.[10]

Finance

The main sources of the borough's income were rents from its estates, tolls from the Hythe, and profits of court, augmented in the 17th century by the farm and other profits of the Dutch Bay Hall. The acquisition of Kingswood (later the Severalls estate) in Mile End in 1535 and of the lands of Barwick's and Heynes's chantries in 1550 greatly increased the borough estates, but some of the chantry lands were sold almost immediately and the rest were mortgaged or let on such a long lease that the rents became insignificant.[11] Total income rose from £127 in 1501–2 to £161 (excluding the proceeds of a special rate for the repair of the harbour) in 1548–9, and to £537 in 1624–5.[12] It seems to have fallen in the later 17th century, and in 1667–8 there was a deficit of £78 as receipts totalled only c. £420, almost all from rents. Income remained well under £500 for the rest of the 17th century, enough to cover ordinary expenditure, but not such extraordinary costs as lawsuits or the acquisition of new charters.[13]

The main items of regular expenditure were the fee farm, which fell from £38 in 1596 to £24 by 1695 as allowance was made for 'taxes',[14] the fees, wages, and liveries of borough officers and servants, and the repair of town buildings and bridges. From 1557 the borough also assumed some responsibility for poor relief.[15] Dinners were provided for the officers and their guests at elections and major court days, and gifts of oysters, candied eryngo, or wine were sent to the borough's patrons and friends at court. In the 17th century freemen were given 8d. a head on election days, in lieu of dinner.[16]

Signs of financial problems appear in the mid 16th century. There was a deficit of £17 on the year 1548–9, and the assembly agreed that no leases or sales of land should be made, or any money paid by the borough, without its consent.[17] That 12 men refused to serve as chamberlain between 1553 and 1557 may be significant;[18] their fines of £3 6s. 8d. each were probably a source of extra income to the borough. Similar fines raised £23 in 1573 and £18 in 1574.[19] In 1577 chamberlains were forbidden to appoint deputies, and each was ordered to make his account at the moot hall on 2 January after the end of his year of office.[20]

In the 17th century the borough was increasingly involved in expensive lawsuits, arising either from the defence of its liberties or from quarrels within the corporation. In 1615 the money in the keykeepers' custody in the town chest was given to the chamberlain to pay for a suit in King's Bench over the town's liberties, and in 1629 a rate was levied to pay the expenses of the suit against Sir Roger Townsend of Wivenhoe over the borough's rights in the Colne.[21] The seizure of

[9] Ibid. ff. 1–4; ibid. MS. Rawl. Essex 1, f. 123; E.R.O., Boro. Mun. vol. of Misc. Papers; cf. ibid. D/B 5 Gb6, p. 275.

[10] E.R.O., D/B 5 Sr103, rot. 36; D/B 5 Gb7, pp. 20–4.

[11] Morant, *Colch.* 158; E.R.O., D/B 5 Gb2, f. 45v.; D/B 5 Cr118, rot. 20d.; Cr138, rot. 10.

[12] Bodl. MS. Rolls Essex 2; B.L. Stowe MS. 829, f. 26v.; E.R.O., D/B 5 Aa1/5.

[13] E.R.O., D/B 5 Aa1/1–26; Aa1/35, ff. 1–90.

[14] *Cal. S.P. Dom.* 1595–7, 162; Bodl. MS. Rawl. Essex

1, f. 137; E.R.O., D/B 5 Aa1/35, ff. 32v., 67, 78.

[15] Above, this chapter, Soc. Structure (Growth of Poverty).

[16] E.R.O., D/B 5 Aa1/1–26; Aa1/35, ff. 1–90.

[17] B.L. Stowe MS. 829, f. 26v.; E.R.O., D/Y 2/2, pp. 19–20.

[18] E.R.O., D/B 5 Cr120, rot. 1; Cr.121, rot. 1; Cr.122, rot. 1; Cr.123, rot. 1.

[19] Ibid. D/B 5 Cr137, rot. 1; Cr138, rot. 1.

[20] Ibid. D/B 5 Gb1, 20 Sept. 1577.

[21] Ibid. D/B 5 Gb2, f. 147v.; Gb3, f. 84.

12 pipes of rape oil in 1630 led to a suit against Henry Barrington which cost £220, and in 1632 the borough resorted to mortgaging lands to raise £300 to cover that and other expenses.[22] Thereafter the borough regularly mortgaged its estates, and in 1655 mortgaged Archbishop Harsnett's library.[23] By 1643 at least part of the capital of one of the borough charities had been spent,[24] probably to cover extraordinary expenses.

After a period of relative stability in the 1660s the borough entered a prolonged period of financial difficulty when it was forced to pay Sir John Shaw £356 compensation for his removal as recorder in 1677.[25] The charters of 1684 and 1688 added to the borough's expenses. Already in 1680, in an effort to improve its regular income, the assembly had set up a committee to oversee the collection of rents, and in 1688 the chamberlains for the previous 16 years were all ordered to produce their accounts.[26] In December 1687 the profits of the Dutch Bay Hall were assigned to the chamberlain as security for his expenditure in a time of political uncertainty.[27] The £328 spent on the charter of 1693 was advanced by Sir Isaac Rebow, on the security of the Dutch Bay Hall. The hall was mortgaged for £100 in 1696, a sum increased to £150 in 1699 and to £500 in 1701.[28] In 1697 efforts were made to recover 'ancient fees, tolls, and duties'.[29] Despite further attempts between 1703 and 1709 to increase the efficiency of rent collection and to audit the chamberlain's accounts carefully, the interest on a £300 mortgage on Borough fields was unpaid in 1705.[30] In 1706 the borough's creditors were asked to present their demands in writing; money to pay them and later creditors was raised by further mortgages, and by the sale of freedoms.[31] In 1712 the assembly mortgaged the Severalls estate at Mile End for £1,000 to cover the costs of a lawsuit, and raised a further £70 from other borough lands for 'necessary expenses'.[32]

Courts

Courts were held by the bailiffs or mayor and the aldermen on Mondays and Thursdays, the Monday court known as the hundred until 1522 and the lawhundred thereafter, the Thursday as the foreign court. General lawhundreds, courts leet, were held three times a year until 1589.[33] The Monday court was apparently for freemen, the Thursday one for 'foreigners', but otherwise there was little distinction between them. The Monday court heard a few pleas concerning real property, and officers were elected there. Regulations were made in 1559 to speed the court process, and in 1574 the assembly drew up a rota of aldermen, four a week, to hold the courts.[34] In 1592 regulations tightened the court rules to provide quicker justice and to make the collection of fines and amercements more efficient.[35] By 1587 the court usually adjourned for the whole of September, presumably because of the borough elections, but might be held that month if necessary.[36] Attorneys were formally admitted to practice in the courts.[37]

The 1635 charter confirmed the borough's cognizance of all pleas, real, personal, and mixed, including the possessory assizes, and pleas of debt, covenant, detinue,

22 Ibid. D/B 5 Gb3, ff. 93, 108v., 111v.–112.
23 e.g. ibid. ff. 154, 229v.; Gb4, f. 135.
24 Ibid. D/B 5 Ab1/15.
25 Glines, 'Politics and Govt. in Colch.' 147–8, 164–5; E.R.O., D/B 5 Gb5, f. 134v.   26 E.R.O., D/B 5 Gb5, ff. 172v., 299–300.
27 Ibid. ff. 283v., 285.
28 Ibid. D/B 5 Gb6, pp. 12–13, 97, 176, 237.
29 Ibid. p. 111.
30 Ibid. pp. 280, 307–8, 318, 385, 550.
31 Ibid. pp. 341, 420; D/B 5 Gb7, ff. 8–10, 13.
32 Ibid. D/B 5 Gb6, p. 436.
33 The following section is based on E.R.O., D/B 5 Cr82–160; D/B 5 Cb1/2–23; D/B 5 Cb2/3–34; ibid. draft catalogue of Ct. R. and Ct. Bks.
34 E.R.O., D/B 5 Cr124, rot. 16; D/B 5 R7, f. 261.
35 Ibid. D/B 5 Gb1, 7 Aug. 1592.
36 Ibid. D/Y 2/7, pp. 227–8; D/Y 2/8, p. 339.
37 Ibid. D/B 5 Gb1, 17 June, 1591; 7 Aug. 1592; 25 Sept. 1598.

account, and trespass,[38] and the provisions were repeated in all other 17th-century charters. In the later 17th century, however, business in both the Monday and the Thursday courts declined, perhaps because of their cumbersome procedure. Although both courts could hear pleas of debt, in 1689 the borough attempted unsuccessfully to acquire a 'court of conscience' for the recovery of debts under 40s. 'according to the rules and methods used within the City of London'.[39]

From 1516 or earlier sessions of the peace were held by the borough J.P.s. From 1521 their proceedings were entered on the borough court rolls, but from 1576 there were separate sessions rolls. The borough sessions had all the powers of a quarter sessions court, and dealt with felonies and other offences committed in Colchester.[40]

The 1635 charter confirmed the mayor's right, exercised from 1493 or earlier, to hold an admiralty court weekly on Thursdays, but also confirmed the admiral's jurisdiction in the borough.[41] In 1588 the bailiffs had disputed the jurisdiction of the newly appointed admiral over the town and its liberty, and although by 1594 they seem to have accepted at least his rights to goods washed ashore, during a dispute with the Colne fishermen in 1630 they again claimed exemption from his jurisdiction.[42] The Colchester admiralty court dealt mainly with fishing offences and with forestalling the oyster market at the Hythe.[43]

Parliamentary Representation

The two M.P.s were elected by the bailiffs, aldermen, and councillors[44] from the 1550s or earlier until 1628 when, after a disputed election, the House of Commons opened the franchise to all free burgesses.[45] The small size of the Tudor electorate made control easy, but nevertheless one M.P. was usually a local man. In 1529 the earl of Oxford procured the election of his councillor Richard Rich; in 1555 the bailiffs, as instructed, elected Sir Francis Jobson.[46] In 1584 the assembly agreed to give Sir Francis Walsingham the nomination of both the borough M.P.s, and duly elected the two men he wanted.[47]

The opposition of the freemen seems to have prevented Robert Radcliffe, earl of Sussex, and Henry Hobart from getting their candidates elected in 1625. Despite the extension of the franchise in 1628, Robert Rich, earl of Warwick, was able to establish his control over the borough that year, but Henry Rich, Lord Holland, was unable to arrange the election of his friend Sir Thomas Ingram in 1640.[48] Later in 1640 the sitting M.P.s, Harbottle Grimston and Sir William Masham, with Robert Rich, Lord Rich, successfully urged the borough to elect Sir Thomas Barrington, who would otherwise have caused a contested election for the county seats.[49]

In 1654 the election was contested for the first time, John Maidstone defeating Col. Goffe by 102 burgesses' votes to 98. Attempts to reduce the electorate to the corporation led to a double election in 1656 when the mayor, aldermen, and councillors elected Henry Laurence, Lord President of the Council, and John

---

[38] *Colch. Charters*, 98–100.

[39] E.R.O., D/B 5 Gb5, ff. 313, 319.

[40] J. Samaha, *Law and Order in Hist. Perspective*, 103 n.

[41] *Colch. Charters*, 99–100; above, Medieval Colch. (Boro. Govt., Courts).

[42] B.L. Lansdowne MS. 157, f. 305; ibid. Add. MS. 12505, f. 424; ibid. Stowe MS. 835, ff. 83–4; E.R.O., D/Y 2/2, p. 157; D/Y 2/8, pp. 341–2.

[43] E.R.O., D/Y 2/2, p. 153; B.L. Stowe MS. 835, f. 91.

[44] e.g. E.R.O., D/B 5 R2, f. 26v.; D/B 5 Gb1 4 Nov. 1588; B.L. Stowe MS. 841, f. 55.

[45] E.R.O., D/B 5 Gb3, f. 70; D. Hirst, *Representative of the People?* 199–201.

[46] E.R.O., D/B 5 Cr99, rot. 1d.; D/Y 2/7, p. 11.

[47] Ibid. D/B 5 Gb1, 26 Oct., 2 Nov. 1584.

[48] Ibid. D/Y 2/4, pp. 26–7, 35–9; Hirst, *Representative of the People?* 134; J. K. Gruenfelder, *Influence in Early Stuart Elections 1604–1640*, 11, 158.

[49] E.R.O., D/Y 2/8, p. 73; D/Y 2/9, p. 53.

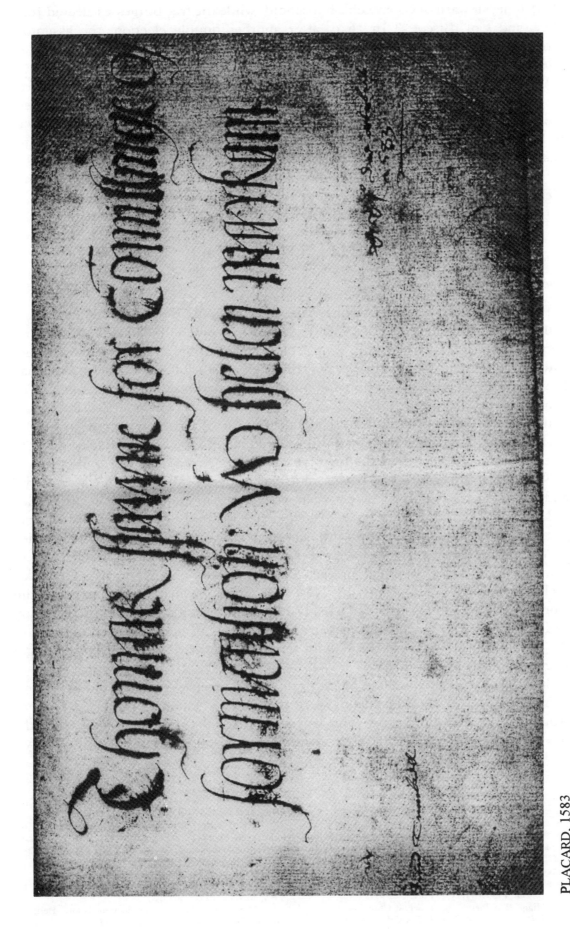

PLACARD, 1583
worn by Thomas Faune, being paraded through the streets in a tumbrel as a punishment for
'fornication'

Maidstone, steward of Cromwell's household, while the free burgesses elected John Shaw and Col. Biscoe.[50] In 1659, after another double election, the assembly petitioned the Committee for Privilege and Election for election by mayor, aldermen, and council only.[51]

After 1660, when Harbottle Grimston and John Shaw were returned, the free burgesses' vote was not disputed. The elections of 1679 and 1681 were contested, and polls were taken.[52] By 1706 the creation of freemen had become an issue at parliamentary as at borough elections. In 1710 the election of Sir Thomas Webster was overturned on petition, and in 1714 William Gore and Nicholas Corsellis successfully petitioned against the election of Sir Isaac Rebow and Sir Thomas Webster, claiming that 235 of their opponents' votes had been invalid.[53]

RELIGIOUS LIFE

The Reformation

Traditional forms of religious observance focusing upon the parish church were still in the ascendant among the majority of townspeople in the early 16th century. Bequests were made for the maintenance of chapels, guilds, chantries, altars, statues and for requiem masses and prayers for the dead.[54] In 1506, for example, alderman John Bardfield endowed an obit for himself, his parents, his two wives and all Christians for 100 years.[55] Three perpetual chantries were established in the late 15th century and another as late as 1523; major work was carried out on several parish churches c. 1500,[56] and the town granted land to the Crutched friars in 1516 to endow a mass 'for the further prosperity of the town'.[57]

Nevertheless, the town had been a centre of Lollardy in the early 15th century[58] and the heresy reappeared c. 1500 when it revived nationally. Six Colchester men did penance at St. Paul's Cross in 1506 and two abjured Colchester heretics were burnt at Smithfield in 1511.[59] In 1527 a heretical group in north-east Essex included 19 men and 14 women from Colchester, many of them from the upper levels of town society. They preached in each others' houses and read English books, including Wyclif's Bible and the New Testament, which they obtained from London.[60] Such groups provided a ready-made organization for the early reception and distribution of Lutheran books in Colchester,[61] although the identification of the author of the Mathews Bible with Thomas Mathews, a Lollard fishmonger from the town, seems unlikely.[62]

St. Botolph's priory was dissolved in 1536, the two friaries in 1538, and St. John's abbey in 1539. Most of their lands were acquired by Thomas Audley, later Lord Audley, Francis Jobson, and John Lucas.[63] Through Audley's intervention the town gained the lands of St. Helen's guild and Eleanor's chantry in St. Mary's

[50] Ibid. D/B 5 Gb4, ff. 51v., 112v.–114v., 145v.–146.

[51] B.L. Stowe MS. 636, ff. 78–82.

[52] E.R.O., D/B 5 Gb5, ff. 156, 181.

[53] Ibid. D/Y 2/2, pp. 341–3; Boro. Mun., 'Colch. MSS.', ff. 4 and v., 19v.–28.

[54] Above, Med. Colch. (Townspeople); L. Higgs, 'Lay Piety in the Borough of Colch., 1485–1558' (Univ. of Michigan Ph.D. thesis, 1983), 141–54.

[55] P.R.O., PROB 11/15, f. 139v.

[56] Higgs, 'Lay Piety', 104–5; below, Churches.

[57] E.R. xlvi. 85–6; E.R.O., D/B 5 Cr87, rot. 8.

[58] Above, Med. Colch. (Townspeople).

[59] J. E. Oxley, Reformation in Essex to the Death of Mary, 5–6.

[60] V.C.H. Essex, ii. 21; L. & P. Hen. VIII, iv (2), pp. 1481, 1788–91, 1844–5, 1859, 1869, 1875, 1984; A. Hudson, Premature Reformation, 477–9; E.A.T. 3rd ser. xv. 84–5; Oxley, Reformation in Essex, 7–10.

[61] A. G. Dickens, Reformation Studies, 376–7.

[62] E.R. xliii. 1–6, 82–7, 155–62, 227–34; xliv. 40–2; lvi. 73–4; E.A.T. 3rd ser. xv. 85.

[63] Above, this chapter, Introduction; below, Religious Houses; Outlying Parts (West Donyland).

church to refound the grammar school.[64] At St. John's in 1534 some monks temporarily refused to take the oath of fealty and the sub-prior called the King's council heretics. The abbot, Thomas Marshall or Beche, took little care to conceal his views against the royal supremacy and the abbey's possible dissolution and was executed at Colchester in 1539.[65]

Many priests were also hostile to the Henrician Reformation. John Wayne, rector of St. James's, and Dr. Thyrstell, at the Grey friars, urged their hearers in 1534 to ignore new books 'of the king's print', probably the propaganda tracts *The Glass of Truth* and the *Articles of the Council*.[66] In 1535 the curate of St. Nicholas's was presented in the borough court for praying for the pope and cardinals and reading a book in church called 'le sentence' which emphasized the authority of Rome.[67] That year at Lexden the rector was fined for stating that 'the blood of Hailes is the blood of Jesus Christ', and the curate in 1538 for teaching the 'paternoster'. Other clergy were presented between 1527 and 1545 for loose morals and not proclaiming royal statutes.[68]

In contrast, the townspeople appear to have readily accepted government policy. Church goods had been sold by 1534 at St. Mary's-at-the-Walls and by 1548 at St. Botolph's, St. James's, and St. Martin's.[69] A will of 1538 contained a protestant preamble and there was a swift decline in bequests to parish churches and the high altar, as gifts to the poor became more important. Requiem masses had apparently lost much of their popularity before 1547, the townspeople increasingly favouring funeral sermons.[70] By 1548 only two guilds or chantries remained at Colchester, Haynes's and Barwick's, the others having been already dissolved illegally by their patrons. Their lands were sold to the borough in 1550.[71] Audley's influence was probably an important factor in the town's attitude, his own support for reform being indicated by his endowment in his will dated 1544 of a Good Friday sermon in St. Peter's church.[72]

Among the more radical townspeople, old Lollard ideas appear to have merged with new protestant teaching on the sacraments.[73] In 1535 a group of Colchester people denied the sacrament of the altar, one man claiming that the doctrine of transubstantiation was akin to believing 'that the moon is made of a green cheese'; he also believed that gutter water was as good as holy water and that he might as well be buried in the highway as in the churchyard. In the same year the parish clerk of St. Peter's refused to go to confession, and in 1539 he was accused with four others of heretical beliefs about the sacraments.[74] Similar views continued to be propagated in Colchester in the 1540s.[75] In 1546 three Colchester heretics were executed 'to the example and terror of others', a fourth was burnt later, and another would not submit even when faced with the rack.[76]

Colchester was a focal point of opposition to Mary's Catholic government. In 1555 the town was described as 'a harbourer of heretics and ever was' and subjected to diligent searches for protestants.[77] During Mary's reign a total of 23 people were

[64] *L. & P. Hen. VIII*, xiv (2), p. 222; *V.C.H. Essex*, ii. 502; *E.A.T.* 3rd ser. xv. 86–7; below, Education.
[65] *V.C.H. Essex*, ii. 97–100; *Bull. Inst. Hist. Res.* xxxiii. 115–21.
[66] *L. & P. Hen. VIII*, vii. 170; *E.A.T.* 3rd ser. xv. 85.
[67] E.R.O., D/B 5 Cr104, rot. 3.
[68] Ibid. rot. 2d.; Cr105, rot. 5; Cr108, rot. 8d; Cr112, rot. 5; Cr114, rott. 2–3; *E.R.* xlix. 165; *E.A.T.* 3rd ser. xv. 87.
[69] *V.C.H. Essex*, ii. 26–7; below, Churches.
[70] *E.A.T.* 3rd ser. xv. 88–9.
[71] *V.C.H. Essex*, ii. 22–3; *Cal. Pat.* 1549–51, 420–1.

[72] P.R.O., PROB 11/31, f. 4; *E.A.T.* 3rd ser. xv. 87.
[73] Cf. C. Cross, *Church and People 1450–1660*, 70–5; Dickens, *Reformation Studies*, 381–2.
[74] E.R.O., D/B 5 Cr104, rot. 3; *L. & P. Hen. VIII*, xiv (1), pp. 462–3.
[75] e.g. E.R.O., D/B 5 Cr111, rot. 3; *L. & P. Hen. VIII*, xviii (2), p. 331; *E.A.T.* 3rd ser. xv. 90.
[76] *L. & P. Hen. VIII*, xviii (2), p. 331; xxi (1), pp. 417, 550–1, 586, 648; *Acts of P.C.* 1542–7, 418, 464, 485.
[77] *Narratives of the Days of the Reformation* (Camd. Soc. [1st ser.] lxxvii), 212.

burnt in Colchester, including 15 townspeople. Two other local protestants were martyred elsewhere and two more died in prison. The repression at the town was greater than anywhere except London and Canterbury.[78] The burnings consolidated protestant feeling, the ugly disturbances accompanying one set of executions being described as a 'slight insurrection' by the Venetian ambassador in 1555. A local Catholic priest reported that 'The rebels are stout in the town of Colchester. The ministers of the church are hemmed at in the open streets, and called knaves. The blessed sacrament of the alter is blasphemed and railed upon in every alehouse and tavern. Prayer and fasting is not regarded. Seditious talks and news are rife'.[79]

Mary's government was particularly concerned about the activities of protestant clergy and lay preachers in the Colchester district. As early as 1554 some people had been actively dissuading others from attendance at the newly restored mass.[80] One of those responsible was probably Thomas Putto, an Anabaptist tanner of Berechurch and a lay preacher during Edward's reign, who had recanted in 1549 and who had been ordained by Ridley in 1552. At the start of Mary's reign in 1554 he led a group of 20 or more heretics and sacramentarians who mustered on Mile End heath in opposition to the papacy.[81] More dangerous was George Eagles, nicknamed Trudgeover or Trudgeover-the-world, a tailor who became an itinerant preacher in the reign of Edward VI. The heaths around Colchester provided secure hiding places until he was finally apprehended at Colchester at St. Mary Magdalen's fair in 1557. He was hanged, drawn, and quartered at Chelmsford one week later, one of his quarters being sent for display in Colchester market place.[82] Most notable of all was John Pulleyne, who had been deprived of St. Peter-upon-Cornhill in London in 1555 and had then preached secretly in Colchester until he fled to Geneva in 1557.[83]

The bailiffs and aldermen were thanked by the Privy Council for their assistance at executions and in the apprehending of Trudgeover,[84] but that help was probably given as much out of prudence as religious conviction. Some aldermen were vigorous Catholics, such as Robert Maynard, bailiff 1552–3 and 1556–7, 'a special enemy to God's gospel'.[85] Others were protestant in sympathy, such as the bailiff Thomas Dibney, who was brought before the Privy Council for his 'evil behaviour in matters of religion', and had to do penance in two parish churches.[86] Yet other members of the local élite were more circumspect in their religious behaviour, the master and rector of St. Mary Magdalen's hospital combining both protestant and Catholic tenets in his 1557 will.[87] While outwardly complying with government instructions the magistrates were evidently afraid of pressing the persecution too hard lest there should be repercussions after Mary's death. Most of those martyred or presented by town juries came from the middling or lower orders particularly in the cloth trades. In 1557 the bailiffs were criticized for delaying the execution of heretics.[88]

The town apparently polarized into sectarian groups, rival alehouses identifying with the protestant or Catholic cause.[89] There is little sign, however, that Mary's

[78] *E.A.T.* 3rd ser. xv. 92; M. Byford, 'The Price of Protestantism: Assessing the Impact of Religious Change on Elizabethan Essex: the Cases of Heydon and Colch. 1558–94' (Oxford Univ. D.Phil. thesis, 1988), 100, 115–17.

[79] *Cal. S.P. Venetian*, vi (i), p. 45; Byford, 'Price of Protestantism', 115.

[80] *V.C.H. Essex*, ii. 32; *Acts of P.C.* 1552–4, 395.

[81] *Chron. of the Grey Friars of London* (Camd. Soc. [1st ser.] liii), 59; *Wriothesley's Chron.* (Camd. 2nd ser. xx), 12; Byford, 'Price of Protestantism', 113; *Acts of P.C.* 1550–52,

81; E.R.O., D/B 5 Cr122, rot. 4d.; *E.R.* l. 157–62.

[82] Byford, 'Price of Protestantism', 113–14; *Acts of P.C.* 1556–8, 19, 129–31, 142.

[83] Byford, 'Price of Protestantism', 112.

[84] *Acts of P.C.* 1554–6, 153; 1556–58, 130–1.

[85] *E.A.T.* 3rd ser. xv. 90.   [86] *Acts of P.C.* 1554–6, 134, 137.

[87] E.R.O., D/ABW 16/128.

[88] *E.A.T.* 3rd ser. xv. 91; Byford, 'Price of Protestantism', 119–27;*Acts of P.C.* 1556–8, 135, 144.

[89] Byford, 'Price of Protestantism', 118–19.

policies reversed the preference of the majority of Colchester's townspeople for religious reform. Most wills in the period 1554–8 had neutral preambles and they contained no requests for requiem masses and few bequests of traditional form.[90] Indeed, the proximity of the Continent provided both a haven for threatened protestants and an entry point for more radical ideas. When Christopher Vittels of the Family of Love arrived from Delft in 1555 he found a ready audience and allegedly debated the divinity of Christ with servants and husbandmen at a Colchester inn.[91]

The authorities acted with extreme caution after Mary's death. It was not until the day before Elizabeth's coronation that eight people held in the castle gaol on suspicion of supporting Trudgeover were released on bail, except for one man 'very evil in matters of religion'. Elizabeth's ban on unauthorized preaching led Peter Walker, Catholic rector of St. Leonard's church, to be pilloried 'for false seditious tales' early in 1559,[92] and to the arrest of the protestant preachers Pulleyne and Dodman shortly afterwards. Pulleyne and other preachers had swiftly returned from exile to provide protestant services in a town where there was popular demand for the adoption of Reformation principles. From Hock Day 1559 the borough court presented people for non-attendance at divine service, and after Pulleyne was appointed archdeacon of Colchester in December 1559, and rector of Copford in 1560, the borough assembly admitted him to the freedom, waiving the customary fine.[93]

The Elizabethan Settlement

A major problem for the ecclesiastical authorities *c.* 1560 was the lack of an effective protestant ministry for the town. Although a suffragan bishopric of Colchester had been created by Henry VIII, only two bishops were appointed, William More 1536–40 and John Sterne 1592–1607.[94] The loss of income from chantries, confessions, obits and soul-masses, which had improved clerical incomes before the Reformation, meant that Colchester's livings were very poor and often attracted pluralists or poorly qualified priests.[95] A scheme to unify town benefices put forward in 1549 had come to nothing, and several parishes remained vacant after the deprivations of 1554. In November 1560 there was not a single beneficed incumbent in the town, but only two curates at St. Leonard's and St. Peter's. By 1561 there were beneficed incumbents at Mile End and Lexden and 3 curates and 5 lectors.[96] Clerical provision had improved by the 1580s and prophesyings, at first suppressed, had been transformed into exercises for the instruction of Colchester's less learned clergy by 1586, as elsewhere in the diocese.[97] Most of Colchester's parishes remained poor, however, and another plan in 1581 to increase stipends by combining a number of Colchester's parishes came to nothing.[98]

The progress of reform in the first decades of Elizabeth's reign was greatly influenced by the opinions of the townspeople. Pressure from the lower and middling social groups, probably encouraged by Pulleyne, led the assembly to vote

[90] *E.A.T.* 3rd ser. xv. 90–1.

[91] Byford, 'Price of Protestantism', 114; *V.C.H. Essex*, ii. 34; Morant, *Colch.* 50; *Sixteenth Century Jnl.* x. 15–22; *D.N.B.*

[92] Byford, 'Price of Protestantism', 129; *V.C.H. Essex*, ii. 34; *Acts of P.C.* 1556–8, 215; 1558–70, 26, 44, 71.

[93] Byford, 'Price of Protestantism', 130–7; *Acts of P.C.* 1558–70, 89; *V.C.H. Essex*, ii. 34–5; E.R.O., D/B 5 Cr125, rot. 1d.

[94] *L. & P. Hen. VIII*, xiv (2), pp. 151–2; Addenda, i (2), p. 498;

[95] *V.C.H. Essex*, ii. 81; Morant, *Colch.* 81.   [95] Below, Churches.

[96] B. Usher, 'Colch. and Diocesan Administration 1539–1604': copy in E.R.O; Byford, 'Price of Protestantism', 138–40; Morant, *Colch.* 105–7; *E.R.* xlvi. 149, 154.

[97] W. Hunt, *Puritan Movement: Coming of Revolution in an Eng. County*, 94–6; P. Collinson, *Religion of Protestants*, 130; below, Churches.

[98] E.R.O., D/Y 2/7, p. 13; D/B 5 Gb1, 23 Jan. 1581; Morant, *Colch.* 105–7.

for the establishment of a borough preachership in 1562. The post was initially funded by voluntary contributions, both large and small, from a very broad range of Colchester society.[99] The post was held by a succession of influential but extreme protestants, the first of whom, William Cole, in office by 1564, was a fellow of Corpus Christi College, Oxford, and a Marian exile whose protestant credentials were impeccable.[1] After 1568 Cole was succeeded in the preachership by George Withers, former preacher at Bury St. Edmunds, and then by Nicholas Challoner from 1573. Pulleyne was succeeded in the archdeaconry by James Calfhill in 1565 and then by Withers in 1570. All were in the vanguard of reformed opinion and under their powerful influence the Colchester assembly set about creating a 'godly' civic commonwealth.[2]

In 1562 the assembly, probably prompted by Pulleyne and Cole, appointed overseers of church attendance and the borough court attempted to prohibit activities such as trading, gambling, and playing games during divine service. Those measures were probably not sabbatarian in nature but were aimed at largely traditional moral ends, and their widespread acceptance may partly be explained by the reformers' use of the traditional structure of the borough court.[3] Pulleyne did meet with opposition from some townspeople who, while regarding themselves as protestant, objected to his emphasis upon the reform of their personal lives. One woman, angered by the length of protestant sermons and the new subjects on which they touched, claimed that Pulleyne had preached away all the pavements and gravestones in St. Martin's churchyard.[4] Nevertheless, the magistrates' rapid assimilation of the reformers' message is indicated by the special tribunal against fornication, presided over by the bailiffs, aldermen, and archdeacon, held in 1566.[5]

The regulations for behaviour introduced by protestant reformers appear to have been more strictly enforced from the late 1570s, when Colchester entered a new phase of reformation under the guidance of Challoner and Withers.[6] Greater emphasis was placed upon the sanctity of the Lord's day rather than just the control of activity during divine service. In 1578 the assembly prohibited business or revelry on pardon Sunday (the fair day of St. Dennis's fair). As sabbatarianism was a subject of dispute in the Dedham classis in the late 1580s, and did not become a firm mark of the Calvinist tradition in England until 1600, it appears to have developed relatively early at Colchester.[7] In the same period the regulation of moral behaviour, especially sexual misconduct, grew more intense in the town. From 1576 new tribunals enquired into both the consumption of meat in Lent and the offences of prostitutes and fornicators. Persons convicted of adultery frequently received the traditional punishment of being paraded through the streets in a tumbrel. Persistent sexual delinquents were whipped, while drunkards and blasphemers were placed in the stocks.[8] By the 1580s alehouses had come under strict regulation, and searches were made to identify people engaged in profane activities.[9]

Many of the local clergy and townspeople adopted advanced protestant opinions that went beyond the Elizabethan settlement. Thomas Upcher, the extreme

[99] Byford, 'Price of Protestantism', 143–6, 155; E.R.O., D/B 5 R5, ff. 12v., 86; below, this chapter, this section (Common Preacher).

[1] Byford, 'Price of Protestantism', 162–4; *D.N.B.*

[2] Byford, 'Price of Protestantism', 164, 174–6, 310–11; Collinson, *Religion of Protestants*, 170–3.

[3] Byford, 'Price of Protestantism', 150–3, 176; E.R.O., Boro. Mun., Misc. Papers (formerly Sess. R. 20), rot. 11; ibid. Q/SR 171, f. 61d.

[4] Byford, 'Price of Protestantism', 165–7.

[5] E.R.O., D/B 5 R5, ff. 12v., 49; Byford, 'Price of Protestantism', 146–8.

[6] e.g. E.R.O., D/B 5 Cr141, rott. 2d., 3d.; Cr143, rott. 2, 2d.

[7] P. Collinson, *Godly People*, 429–32, 438–9.

[8] Byford, 'Price of Protestantism', 385–7, 397; E.R.O., D/B 5 Cr140, rott. 9, 10d.; Cr141, rot. 13; Cr142, rot. 5; Cr144, rot. 13d.; Cr145, rott. 23, 31d.; Cr152, rot. 14d.

[9] *E.R.* lii. 89–95; above, this chapter (Social Structure).

protestant incumbent of St. Leonard's, defended his refusal to wear a surplice by claiming that his congregation opposed its use,[10] and Robert Holmes, rector of St. James's, was presented before the borough court for stating that the surplice was 'a superstitious thing from the pope'.[11] Several Colchester incumbents became members of the clandestine Dedham classis, formed in 1582, which sometimes met in the town.[12] Zealous laymen abandoned their parish churches for others where the doctrine was more to their taste: three parishioners of St. Nicholas's went elsewhere for instruction because of the 'simplicity' of their minister, while another incumbent appealed to the Dedham classis for a ruling 'that a pastor should have his own people' after he had lost his congregation to the rival attraction of the common preacher.[13] By the turn of the century refusals to attend church, to have children baptized, or to kneel for communion were common, while many of the parish churches were in poor repair, lacking equipment, fittings, vestments, and books.[14]

The new protestant morality was probably popular in nature rather than imposed from above. Wills from the late 16th century frequently record gifts for the town preacher, for funeral and other sermons, and for the poor.[15] Yet there had been far more of a consensus in the town during the first decade of Elizabeth's reign than during the late 1570s and the 1580s. The 'godly' party received a considerable setback when Benjamin Clere and his supporters were displaced from the town government after their dispute with John Lone in 1576, which had revealed their own weaknesses in learning and conformity and highlighted Clere's role in the Marian persecution.[16] The dispute revealed a division within the protestant ranks between the extremists and the moderates who emphasized Christian charity.[17] The reformers continued to be opposed by townspeople who could probably be classified as among the profane, such as the two men caught playing cards in the King's Head at the time of divine service in 1589.[18]

Another source of opposition came from those townspeople who remained faithful to Catholicism. The Audleys' house at Berechurch became an important recusant centre; another prominent recusant was Richard Cousins, keeper of the White Hart.[19] In 1578, as the repression of Catholics in East Anglia gathered momentum, the bailiffs wrote to the Privy Council warning of obstinate recusants in Colchester.[20] Both Catholics and protestants energetically attempted to undermine each other's cause. A London sadler sheltering at Berechurch gave poor men money to persuade them not to attend lectures, presumably those given by Colchester's preacher,[21] while in 1587 a captured Catholic priest was forced to take part in a disputation in the moot hall with the town preacher in order to reveal the superiority of protestant learning.[22]

A few cases of witchcraft had been reported before the Reformation: in 1532, for example, a smith's wife was accused of practising magic 'to make folks believe they

[10] Byford, 'Price of Protestantism', 142.
[11] E.R.O., D/B 5 Sb2/4, f. 78; D/B 5 Cr150, rot. 32.
[12] *Presbyterian movement in the reign of Eliz.* (Camd. 3rd ser. viii), 28–74; *V.C.H. Essex*, ii. 39 n.; Smith, *Eccl. Hist. Essex*, 12.
[13] Collinson, *Godly People*, 9–10.
[14] J. R. Davis, 'Colch. 1600–1662: Politics, Religion and Officeholding in an Eng. Provincial Town' (Brandeis Univ. Ph.D. thesis, 1980), 85–9; below, Churches.
[15] F. G. Emmison, *Elizabethan Life: Wills of Essex Gentry and Merchants*, 249, 273–4, 281, 292, 298–9, 312, 319; F. G.

Emmison, *Essex Wills*, iii. 215–16, 232, 266, 268, 358–9; iv. 105, 122, 142, 146, 153–4, 160, 166.
[16] Byford, 'Price of Protestantism', 194–284; above, this chapter (Boro. Govt.).
[17] Byford, 'Price of Protestantism', 259–68, 277–8.
[18] E.R.O., D/B 5 Sb2/5, f. 109v.
[19] Below, Roman Catholicism; Byford, 'Price of Protestantism', 158–62.
[20] E.R.O., D/Y 2/5, p. 19; *Religious Dissent in East Anglia*, ed. E. S. Leedham-Green, 14–15.
[21] *Essex Recusant*, v. 84.
[22] Byford, 'Price of Protestantism', 335.

should have a silly (lucky) plough'.[23] By Elizabeth's reign the potentially malevolent aspects of such activity were more greatly feared. At least a dozen accusations were made against Colchester people, mostly women, who were thought to have harmed people or animals through magic.[24] Although one woman admitted diabolic possession, many cases apparently derived from popular reliance upon white magic and cunning folk. In 1573 one man confessed he had sent to 'Mother Humfrey' to lift a curse on his hogs, while in 1582 a woman who denied witchcraft admitted she had learnt a counter-spell from Goodwife George of Abberton. Specialist magical assistance was available in the town: in 1590 a couple from Lawford made a magic ointment to cure their children's sickness on the advice of a Colchester physician and in 1598 another Lawford man sent his wife to a cunning man, 'Goodin of Colchester', to help find a stolen horse.[25]

The 17th Century

The growth of separatist sects in Colchester presented a challenge both to the local incumbents and to the common preacher. In 1604 a group of Brownists clashed with Richard Harris, the preacher, whom they denounced as a non-resident and persecutor of God's people. The Brownists may have had some support from within the town government for Harris regarded one alderman as 'a spiteful enemy' and the assembly eventually dismissed him.[26] By the 1610s several separatist congregations existed in the town, among them the conventicle headed by John Wilkinson, who wrote a treatise denouncing infant baptism while in prison in 1613.[27] Nevertheless, the total number of separatists may still have been small, only 11 people in the town being presented for absenting themselves from divine service in 1618.[28] By the 1620s the rise of the Arminian party within the Church of England polarized religious differences in the town. The king's Directions for Preachers of 1622, limiting puritan evangelism, apparently caused a dispute over the choice of common preacher. The bishop's commissary, Dr. Robert Aylett, complained of the factious multitude, 'who will allow no minister but of their own calling and choice'.[29] Two years later a complaint was made to the bailiffs by a townsman that extreme protestants had been arrested and sent away as rebels or soldiers.[30] The archdeaconry court attempted to enforce attendance at church and conformity to Laudian doctrine: a number of people were charged for refusing to kneel at communion,[31] and a Greenstead man was presented in 1627 as an excommunicate, Brownist, and Congregationalist.[32]

Archbishop Laud's orders for the relocation of the communion table and erection of rails were moderately successful: by May 1636 as many as 9 of Colchester's 12 churches had complied and another did so later in the year.[33] Although a number of incumbents had initially refused to give communion at the altar rail, many others supported Laud, and by 1637 only John Knowles, the common preacher, refused to conform and receive communion at the archdeacon's visitation.[34] In contrast, Laud's attempt to undermine the membership of the Dutch reformed church, which had associated itself with the 'godly' or puritan opposition, appears to have

23 E.R.O., D/B 5 Cr101, rot. 9; K. Thomas, *Religion and the Decline of Magic*, 776.

24 E.R.O., D/B 5 Sr3; D/B 5 Sr6; D/B 5 Sb2/5, ff. 85v.–87, 97v., 165v.–166; C. L. Ewen, *Witch-Hunting and Witch Trials*, 284; A. Macfarlane, *Witchcraft in Tudor and Stuart Eng.: a Regional and Comparative Study*, 286–7, 299.

25 Macfarlane, *Witchcraft*, 290, 292; E.R.O., ACA/18, f. 132v.; ACA/24, f. 120v.   26 Davis, 'Colch. 1600–62', 90–1.

27 Ibid. 92.   28 E.R.O., D/B 5 Sr23, rott. 4–6.

29 Ibid. D/Y 2/7, p. 19; Hunt, *Puritan Movement*, 175–6.

30 Ibid. D/Y 2/6, pp. 129, 132–3.

31 Below, Churches.   32 E.R.O., D/ALV 1, f. 72v.

33 Ibid. D/ACA 51, ff. 27v., 51, 61, 78v., 81, 87 and v.; W. Cliftlands, 'The "Well-Affected" and the "Country"' (Essex Univ. Ph.D. thesis, 1987), 225.

34 Below, Churches; Smith, *Eccl. Hist. Essex*, 57.

failed.[35] Neither were the protestant townspeople easily intimidated. James Wheeler, churchwarden of St. Botolph's, refused to rail in the altar, but was excommunicated and imprisoned. He later escaped and fled into exile.[36] About 1635 scandalous verses circulated against Theophilus Roberts, rector of St. Nicholas's, who had erected an altar rail and prosecuted persons refusing to contribute to the cost. The verses suggested that he preached only once a month to little effect, and accused other Laudian clergy, Thomas Newcomen, rector of Holy Trinity, Gabriel Honifold, rector of St. Mary Magdalen's, and William Eyres, rector of Great Horkesley and formerly common preacher, of popery and dissolute life.[37] Clergy who did conform to Laud's injunctions were liable to lose their congregations, the disaffected protestants attending lectures elsewhere.[38] Laud's policies apparently failed to undermine the growth of extremist ideas. As a result the Calvinist Dutch church felt it necessary to reinforce its discipline.[39] In 1640 two Colchester weavers claimed to be the prophets mentioned in Zachariah 4:4 and to have the power to stop rain, turn waters to blood, and smite the earth with plagues. They both died in London of the plague in 1642.[40]

Thomas Newcomen frequently clashed with prominent Colchester puritans, including Samuel Burrows who attempted to prosecute Newcomen for undermining the Elizabethan settlement by refusing to administer the sacrament other than at the altar rail. Burrows was later excommunicated after he had distributed a scandalous libel in three Colchester churches on a Sunday morning, and when Newcomen publicized the sentence shots were fired outside his church.[41] Newcomen was also associated with the High Commission's investigation of John Bastwick in 1634, perhaps because Bastwick had described Newcomen as 'a mad parson' two years earlier.[42] The trial and his subsequent imprisonment turned Bastwick into a reckless pamphleteer, a career which eventually brought him before Star Chamber with Henry Burton and William Prynne in 1637, and a further fine, imprisonment, and the loss of his ears in the pillory.[43] The harsh sentences rebounded on the Laudian party: in Colchester in 1641 a nonconforming linen-draper prosecuted before Aylett informed the court 'it were good or better for the church if there were a thousand more such as Bastwick was',[44] and Newcomen only narrowly escaped being beaten to death by Colchester rioters in 1642.[45]

The Civil War committees for scandalous and plundered ministers apparently sequestrated six Colchester incumbents: Cock at St. Giles's, Jarvis at Greenstead, Nettles at Lexden, Honifold at St. Mary Magdalen's, Newcomen at Holy Trinity, and Goffe at St. Leonard's. Thomas Eyres was stripped of Great Horkesley but allowed to keep Mile End.[46] Under presbyterian organization the town constituted one of the four sub-divisions of Thurstable classis, but only three ministers, from 1648, are known: Robert Harmer, the town preacher, Alexander Piggot at St. Leonard's, and James Wyersdale at Lexden.[47] There was by then little support for presbyterianism among the townspeople, who apparently preferred the independent congregational churches. Even incumbents not sequestered by parliament received

[35] *Religious Dissent*, ed. Leedham-Green, 60.
[36] Cliftlands, 'The "Well-Affected"', 227–8; *V.C.H. Essex*, ii. 53–4.
[37] Below, Churches (St. Nicholas); *Cal. S.P. Dom.* 1631–3, 492.
[38] Cliftlands, 'The "Well-Affected"', 233, 236.
[39] *Religious Dissent*, ed. Leedham-Green, 64–7.
[40] *False Prophets Discovered, . . . Lives and Deaths of Two Weavers late of Colch.* (1642, repr. 1844): copy in E.R.O.
[41] *Cal. S.P. Dom.* 1636–7, 265; Bodl. MS. Tanner 70, ff. 107–11; Smith, *Eccl. Hist. Essex*, 413–16; Hunt, *Puritan*

Movement, 276.
[42] E.R.O., D/B 5 Sb1/4, 3 Mar. 1631/2.
[43] *Cal. S.P. Dom.* 1640–1, 319–20; F. M. Condick, 'Life and works of Dr. John Bastwick (1595–1654)' (London Univ. Ph.D. thesis, 1982); *V.C.H. Essex*, ii. 53; *D.N.B.*
[44] *Cal. S.P. Dom.* 1641–3, 520.
[45] Above, this chapter (Intro.).
[46] Smith, *Eccl. Hist. Essex*, 125–7.
[47] *Division of Essex into Classes* (1648), 21: copy in E.C.L. Colch.; *V.C.H. Essex*, ii. 61.

rough treatment; in 1647 there were tumults all day in Lexden church when a group of extremists sang all 176 verses of Psalm 119 to stop the presbyterian minister, James Wyersdale, from preaching.[48] By 1652 the elders of the Dutch church believed that most of the inhabitants of Colchester were great Independents who despised presbyterian government,[49] and in 1656 Evelyn described Colchester as 'swarming with sectaries'.[50]

When Henry Barrington's 'godly' Cromwellian party took control of borough government in 1647 they ordered the constables to enforce strict sabbatarianism.[51] Henry Batchelor, by will proved c. 1647, gave to trustees rents of £60 charged on lands in Southminster to augment the stipends of three 'common preachers of God's word resident in Colchester'.[52] In the same year all property holders were asked to contribute a rate of 1s. in the pound towards the maintenance of 'godly, orthodox ministers'. Similar rates were charged in 1650, 1651, 1653, and 1654, but the system apparently lapsed after the Restoration.[53] To ensure frequent sermons the town authorities brought in ministers such as Ralph Josselin, rector of Earls Colne, who preached in 1646, 1650, and 1652. A plan of 1650 to reduce the number of parishes in the town from 12 to 4, each with a preaching minister, had apparently been abandoned by 1660.[54] Religious radicals visited the town, such as Lawrence Clarkson, the Baptist seeker, in the late 1640s, the Quaker James Parnell in 1650, 1652, and 1655, and the Baptist Thomas Tillam and the Fifth Monarchist Henry Jessey in 1655.[55] Some moderates were prosecuted: John Vickers was imprisoned for a sermon in Holy Trinity against regicide in 1654.[56]

During the disturbed years of the interregnum there appears to have been an increase in witchcraft accusations. A man who cut the tail off a neighbour's cat in 1651 was released from possession only after a lock of his hair had been burnt.[57] The same year John Locke, a 'practitioner of physic' from Ipswich, claimed to be able to recover goods 'by a figure in an almanac'. He also cured John Lawcell by 'some inward medicines', although Lawcell's wife had already paid £5 to a baymaker who made the strange claim that he had killed one man already and must kill another before he could cure Lawcell.[58]

In 1676 there were said to be 170 nonconformists and 2 papists as against 1,891 conformists, about twice the national average of dissenters.[59] Several post-Restoration aldermen and other members of influential Colchester families retained strong nonconformist sympathies.[60] In 1684 the families of the aldermen Ralph Creffield and Nathaniel Laurence were alleged to attend conventicles. At the bishop's visitation Creffield was reported to have encouraged the crowd to shout 'here comes the pope in his lawn sleeves' and to have refused to prosecute those who did not attend divine service.[61] In 1663 the Colchester Quakers, having been locked out of their meeting house by the mayor, held illegal meetings in private houses, led by the former alderman John Furley.[62] The following year a Quaker gathering was dispersed, with great difficulty, by the militia.[63] As late as 1686

48 E.R.O., D/B 5 Sb2/9, ff. 7v.–8; Cliftlands, 'The "Well-Affected"', 175, 185–6.
49 Religious Dissent, ed. Leedham-Green, 66.
50 V.C.H. Essex, ii. 61.
51 E.R.O., D/B 5 Gb3, f. 276; above, this section (Boro. Govt.).
52 E.R.O., D/B 5 Gb4, f. 103v.; ibid. Q/RSr3, 25; Char. Com. File.
53 E.R.O., D/B 5 Gb4, ff. 39v., 64v., 90, 115v.; Gb6, f. 219; C.J. vi. 416, 458; Morant, Colch. 106.
54 V.C.H. Essex, ii. 65; Morant, Colch. 106; E.R.O., D/B 5 Gb4, ff. 174, 213, 218.

55 Cliftlands, 'The "Well-Affected"', 169; below, Prot. Nonconf.   56 E.R.O., D/B 5 Sb2/9, f. 88v.
57 Ibid. D/B 5 Gb4, ff. 52v.–53.
58 Ibid. D/B 5 Sb2/9, f. 65 and v.; Ewen, Witch Hunting and Witch Trials, 285.
59 Compton Census, ed. Whiteman, 50; Collinson, Godly People, 27.   60 Above, this chapter (Boro. Govt.).
61 B.L. Stowe MS. 835, ff. 37–43v.; Bodl. MS. Rawl. Essex 1, ff. 113–17, 120–1, 126–8.
62 E.R.O., D/B 5 Sb2/9, f. 132 and v.
63 Cal. S.P. Venetian 1661–4, 286.

Furley was fined £20 for preaching at a meeting house in St. Martin's, an offence for which 10 others were also indicted, including a gentleman, 4 baymakers, 2 merchants, and a labourer.[64] A loyal address to the king in 1696 was signed by 126 Colchester Quakers.[65]

The Common Preacher

The preachership was initially maintained by voluntary contributions from a wide cross-section of Colchester society. There were at least 45 contributors in 1564 and 89 in 1568, giving amounts varying from 1d. a month to 40s. a year. By 1573 a rent of £20 a year from Kingswood heath had been assigned to the preacher's stipend, and later lecturers were maintained by the town, as at Ipswich.[66] The stipend, which soon outstripped the incomes of local incumbents, was probably necessary to attract good candidates from Cambridge. In 1575 Nicholas Challoner was allotted a rent of £40, as was his successor, George Northey.[67] The stipend was raised to £66 13s. 4d. in 1593 on the appointment of Richard Harris and that year an additional preacher at St. Peter's church was maintained by a collection of £20 in South and East wards.[68] The stipend was raised to £100 in 1619, but was often halved in the 17th century when the preacher held a local living and gave one lecture a week in Colchester instead of the normal two.[69] Preachers were sometimes able to negotiate additional annual payments, such as the £10 received by William Eyres for accommodation in 1610 and the £10 granted to Richard Pulley in 1663 to pay him, or an assistant, to read the Prayer Book before the sermon.[70] In the mid 1680s the sermons were provided by a 'combination' of three beneficed town clergy who were paid £1 a sermon.[71] A new preacher appointed in 1700 was financed that year by the £50 fine for the fishery lease.[72]

From the late 16th century or earlier regular weekly sermons were given on Sunday afternoons and Wednesday mornings.[73] In 1620 a curate also read prayers before the Wednesday sermon.[74] At least 30 sermons were given in 1684 by the 'combination' of three local clergymen.[75] In 1597 St. Botolph's was regarded as 'the most convenient and fittest place' for the sermon.[76] By 1610 the sermons were at St. James's on Sundays and St. Botolph's on Wednesdays, but the Wednesday sermon was transferred to St. Peter's when the preacher was appointed to that living in 1630.[77] Although the Wednesday sermon was at St. Nicholas's in 1658 it was more usually at St. Peter's in the later 17th century, while St. James's retained the Sunday sermon.[78]

The assembly's freedom of action in the selection of preachers was affected both by popular demand and by deference to the opinion of the retiring preacher. The extreme protestant George Northey was recommended by Nicholas Challoner on his deathbed in 1580, and in 1635 the outgoing preacher Richard Maden favoured John Knowles, who was duly appointed.[79] Most Colchester preachers were Cambridge-educated puritans, often college fellows. By 1618 a candidate had to be a graduate and was nominated and presented to the bishop of London.[80] The

[64] Hist. MSS. Com. 38, *14th Rep. IX, Round*, p. 275.
[65] E.R.O., D/B 5 Gb6, f. 88.
[66] B.L. Stowe MS. 829, f. 84; E.R.O., D/Y 2/2, pp. 115, 119; Byford, 'Price of Protestantism', 155; Smith, *Eccl. Hist. Essex*, 21.
[67] E.R.O., D/B 5 Cb1/2, f. 269; D/B 5 Gb1, Dec. 1580.
[68] Ibid. D/B 5 Gb1, Mar., Aug. 1593.
[69] Ibid. D/B 5 Gb4, ff. 271v., 310.
[70] Ibid. D/B 5 Gb2, f. 97v.; Gb4, f. 288.
[71] Ibid. D/B 5 Ab1/21–4; D/B 5 Gb5, ff. 201v., 242v.;

for combination lectures, Collinson, *Godly People*, 467–98.
[72] E.R.O., D/B 5 Gb6, f. 214.
[73] Ibid. D/B 5 Gb1, Dec. 1579; Gb2, f. 76v.; Gb4, f. 23v.
[74] Ibid. D/Y 2/2, p. 118.   [75] Ibid. D/B 5 Ab1/21.
[76] Ibid. D/B 5 Gb1, Dec. 1597.
[77] Ibid. D/B 5 Gb2, f. 96v.; *Cal. S.P. Dom.* 1629–31, 258.
[78] E.R.O., D/B 5 Ab1/20; D/B 5 Gb4, ff. 173, 200v., 204v.; Gb5, f. 201v.; Gb6, f. 214.
[79] Ibid. D/Y 2/6, p. 83; D/B 5 Gb3, ff. 144, 146v.
[80] Ibid. D/B 5 Gb2, ff. 169, 173v.

town did take some precautions; for Northey the bailiffs obtained a reference from Clare Hall, Cambridge, while Richard Harris, chaplain to the earl of Essex, had to preach to the assembly before his appointment in 1593.[81] Interested parties lobbied for particular candidates, as did Harbottle Grimston and John Duke, of Ipswich, in favour of Christopher Scott in 1627,[82] but the views of eminent Cambridge divines evidently carried much weight. In 1627 one of the bailiffs travelled to Cambridge to enquire after a 'learned divine' to be common preacher, and other officers were sent on similar errands in 1631, 1632, and 1635.[83]

The pressing need for an effective protestant ministry in Colchester led Bishop Grindal to allow Colchester's first preachers, Cole, Withers, and Challoner, some latitude in matters of conformity. In the 1580s, however, the new bishop, John Aylmer, took a much harder line, and George Northey was suspended and imprisoned for nonconformity in 1583 soon after his appointment. Aylmer recommended a replacement but between 1583 and 1585 the bailiffs attempted to secure Northey's freedom through the influence of William Cole, Sir Thomas Heneage, Sir Francis Walsingham, and the earls of Leicester and Warwick. A compromise seems to have been reached as Northey was apparently restored before his death in 1593.[84]

The stipend of Northey's successor, Richard Harris, was reduced after he had fallen out with some aldermen and he was dismissed in 1608.[85] In 1609–10 the bishop urged the bailiffs to appoint one of the existing underfunded incumbents, but they defiantly selected William Ames, an extreme Calvinist who was already suspended at Cambridge. Ames was forbidden to preach by the bishop and forced into exile in Holland.[86] His replacement, William Eyres, was apparently more acceptable to the bishop but less popular with the townspeople. He continued to claim the preachership after he became rector of Great Horkesley in 1618, interfering with the sermons and leading the local incumbents in opposition to his replacement Francis Liddell.[87] As late as 1627 Richard Maden wanted the matter settled before he would accept the preachership.[88]

Maden's appointment was also complicated by the unsuccessful attempt of the earl of Warwick and Harbottle Grimston, the recorder, to secure the appointment of a presbyterian candidate. In 1631 Maden was temporarily replaced by William Bridge, who was forced to flee to Holland after being excommunicated for puritanism.[89] To comply with Laud's regulation that lecturers must hold a benefice in their towns, Maden was presented to St. Peter's vicarage.[90] In 1633 the preachership was one of only three in Essex that survived Laud's inquiry into the conformity of lecturers.[91] On Maden's death that year Laud pressed, perhaps as a conciliatory gesture, the claims of two prominent London puritans associated with the earl of Warwick, but Maden's own choice, John Knowles, succeeded him. Knowles was a Cambridge puritan with considerable public influence, and he clashed with Laud in 1637 over the vacant mastership of Colchester grammar school. At a visitation that year it was reported that Knowles did not wear a surplice, say prayers for the king, or take and give communion. Soon afterwards Laud

[81] Ibid. D/Y 2/6, p. 83; D/B 5 Gb1, Aug. 1593.
[82] Ibid. D/Y 2/4, p. 139; D/Y 2/8, p. 19.
[83] Ibid. D/B 5 Gb3, ff. 61v., 62, 99, 109v., 115, 144.
[84] Ibid. D/Y 2/6, pp. 81–3, 85, 87, 89, 91–2, 95, 99, 105, 107, 121, 153; Smith, *Eccl. Hist. Essex*, 24; Byford, 'Price of Protestantism', 327–41.
[85] E.R.O., D/B 5 Gb2, ff. 55v., 68; Davis, 'Colch. 1600–62', 95–7, 101.

[86] E.R.O., D/Y 2/2, p. 123; D/B 5 Gb2, ff. 76v., 96v.; *D.N.B.*
[87] E.R.O., D/B 5 Gb2, f. 179; D/Y 2/4, p. 139; D/Y 2/2, p. 118; Smith, *Eccl. Hist. Essex*, 23–4; Davis, 'Colch. 1600–62', 100–1.
[88] E.R.O., D/Y 2/4, p. 183; D/B 5 Gb3, f. 72.
[89] Davis, 'Colch. 1600–62', 186–8; *D.N.B.*
[90] *Cal. S.P. Dom.* 1629–31, 258.   [91] Ibid. 1631–3, 352.

revoked his licence and Knowles left for New England in 1639.[92] The preachership was apparently less influential in the later 17th century, although it was held by the presbyterian divine Owen Stockton (1657–62).[93]

Colchester's common preachers played a pivotal role in the religious and cultural life of the community and bore much responsibility for the town's continuing tradition of nonconformity. As the majority of church livings were in the gift of local families such as the Audleys and Lucases, the preachership was the only way that the townspeople could guarantee themselves godly instruction.[94] The preachers' popularity is revealed by the many small legacies they received in wills and by the frequent accompanying request that they provide a funeral sermon.[95] Some preachers apparently became well integrated into the social life of the town: Withers married into a Colchester family shortly before his appointment; Challoner married the daughter of alderman Benjamin Clere; and Northey later married Challoner's widow.[96] The preachers' views met with some opposition: in 1566 a man claimed that Cole should be deprived because he did not wear a tippet and square cap; another disagreed with Challoner about predestination.[97] Such doctrinal disputes may have grown sharper with the growth of separatist sects in Colchester during the 17th century. Preachers were also criticized when they addressed non-religious matters from the pulpit, and their involvement in reforming the town's moral life led to disputes with those townspeople who objected to the stricter regulation and harsher punishments that accompanied 'godly' rule.[98]

THE BURNING OF THE PROTESTANT JOHN LAURENCE
29 March, 1555

92 Davis, 'Colch. 1600–62', 188. 93 *D.N.B.*

94 Below, Churches.

95 e.g. Emmison, *Elizabethan Life: Wills of Essex Gentry and Merchants*, 273, 281, 292, 298, 312; E.R.O., D/ACR 96; D/ABW 21/168.

96 Byford, 'Price of Protestantism', 174, 313, 316.

97 E.R.O., D/B 5 R5, f. 76v.; Byford, 'Price of Protestantism', 273.

98 e.g. E.R.O., D/B 5 Sb2/3, ff. 123, 138v.; above, this section (Eliz. Settlement).

BAILIFFS AND MAYORS OF COLCHESTER, 1500 - 1714

The bailiffs, and later the mayors, took office at Michaelmas (29 September) and served until Michaelmas the following year. Their names were recorded in the borough court rolls which survive as a series from 1509/10 to 1740/1 (E.R.O., D/B 5 Cr82 onwards). The names for the years 1500 to 1563 were also entered in the Oath Book (E.R.O., D/B 5 R1), and those for the years from 1576 were recorded in the Assembly Books (E.R.O., D/B 5 Gb1 - 7). Lists of bailiffs and mayors have been published by H. Harrod, *Report on the Records of the Borough of Colchester*, and by George Rickword, *Bailiffs and Mayors of Colchester*. Harrod's list is substantially correct; Rickword's contains a number of errors. The following list is based on Harrod's list, corrected where necessary from the Oath Book, Assembly Book, and other records; full references for all such corrections are given in *V.C.H. Essex*, vol. ix, 377--9.

Bailiffs 1485 - 1634

1485 Thomas Jobson and John Upcher
1486 Richard Marks and Thomas Christmas
1487 Thomas Jobson and Richard Hervey (died in office, succeeded by Richard Plomer)
1488 Richard Haynes and Richard Halke (died in office, succeeded by Thomas Christmas)
1489 John Upcher and Richard Barker
1490 Thomas Jobson and John Bardfield
1491 Thomas Christmas the elder and Nicholas Clere
1492 John Upcher and John Bardfield
1493 Richard Marks and Thomas Christmas the elder
1494 Richard Haynes and Richard Barker
1495 Thomas Christmas the elder and John Thirsk
1496 Richard Haynes and Richard Barker
1497 Thomas Christmas the elder and Thomas Christmas the younger
1498 John Sweyn and John Breton
1499 Thomas Christmas the elder and Richard Barker (died in office, succeeded by Thomas Jobson)
1500 Thomas Christmas the younger and John Sweyn
1501 Robert Cowbridge and John John
1502 John Sweyn and Robert Best
1503 Thomas Christmas and John Mayking
1504 John Sweyn and Richard Pack
1505 John Bardfield (replaced by Thomas Christmas) and William Bennett
1506 Thomas Christmas and John Sweyn
1507 Robert Cowbridge and William Bennett
1508 [unknown]
1509 Thomas Christmas and John Sweyn
1510 John Mayking and Richard Pack
1511 John Sweyn and John Reynold
1512 John Smallpiece and John Bryan
1513 John Sweyn and John Clere
1514 John Smallpiece and John Colle
1515 Thomas Christmas and John Reynold
1516 John Mayking and John Christmas
1517 Thomas Christmas and John Coggeshall
1518 John Clere and John Colle
1519 Thomas Christmas (died in office, succeeded by John Christmas)[58] and William Debenham
1520 John Clere and John Colle
1521 Ambrose Lowth and William Jobson
1522 John Bradman and John Flingaunt
1523 John Mayking and John Colle
1524 John Clere and John Coggeshall

1525 John Christmas and Christopher Hammond
1526 Ambrose Lowth and John Neve
1527 Thomas Flingaunt and John Smallpiece
1528 John Mayking and John Coggeshall
1529 John Colle and William Becket
1530 Ambrose Lowth and John Neve
1531 John Christmas and John Mayking
1532 John Clere and Thomas Cook
1533 Thomas Flingaunt and John Smallpiece
1534 John Colle and William Becket
1535 John Christmas and John Neve
1536 John Clere and Thomas Flingaunt
1537 Robert Brown and William Thurston
1538 John Christmas and Thomas Cook
1539 John Neve and Robert Leche
1540 Austin Beriff (resigned, replaced by Thomas Flingaunt who died in office and was succeeded by John Christmas) and George Sayer
1541 Benjamin Clere and Robert Brown the younger
1542 Thomas Cook and William Buxton
1543 Robert Brown the elder and Robert Flingaunt
1544 Benjamin Clere and Austin Beriff
1545 Robert Leche and Thomas Reve
1546 George Sayer and Robert Brown the younger
1547 John Christmas and John Best
1548 Benjamin Clere and Robert Flingaunt
1549 Robert Leche and Thomas Dibney
1550 John Beriff and John Stone (died in office, succeeded by Robert Brown)
1551 John Best and William Mott
1552 George Sayer and Robert Maynard
1553 Benjamin Clere and John Maynard
1554 John Beriff and John Dibney
1555 George Sayer and William Strachey
1556 Robert Brown and Robert Maynard
1557 John Best and John Maynard
1558 Benjamin Clere and William Mott
1559 George Sayer and John Best
1560 Robert Brown and Robert Northen
1561 John Maynard and Robert Middleton
1562 Benjamin Clere and Robert Lambert
1563 George Sayer and John Best
1564 Robert Middleton and Richard Northey
1565 Benjamin Clere and Nicholas Clere
1566 John Maynard and Robert Northen
1567 George Sayer and John Best
1568 Robert Middleton and Robert Lambert
1569 Robert Northen and Richard Northey

1570 Benjamin Clere and John Fowle
1571 John Best and Thomas Turner
1572 Robert Lambert and Thomas Laurence
1573 John Pye and William Simpson (resigned, replaced by Robert Middleton)
1574 Thomas Turner and Richard Thurston
1575 Benjamin Clere and Robert Mott
1576 Robert Lambert and Thomas Laurence
1577 John Pye and John Hunwick
1578 Richard Thurston and Nicholas Clere (died in office, succeeded by William Turner)
1579 Robert Mott and Thomas Cook
1580 Thomas Laurence and Richard Lambert
1581 Robert Lambert and John Pye
1582 John Hunwick and John Bird
1583 William Turner and Robert Bird
1584 Robert Mott and Thomas Cook
1585 Thomas Laurence and Richard Lambert
1586 John Pye and William Earnesby
1587 John Bird and Thomas Barlow
1588 Robert Bird (died in office, succeeded by Thomas Laurence) and Martin Bessell
1589 Robert Mott and Thomas Cook
1590 John Pye and Thomas Reynold
1591 Thomas Laurence and Ralph Northey
1592 Thomas Hazlewood and William Dibney
1593 John Hunwick (died in office, succeeded by Thomas Hazlewood)[62] and John Bird
1594 Robert Mott and Martin Bessell
1595 Thomas Hazlewood and Henry Osborne
1596 Ralph Northey and Thomas Ingram
1597 Thomas Reynold and William Turner
1598 Richard Simnell and Robert Wade
1599 Robert Mott and Thomas Heckford
1600 Martin Bessell and Henry Osborne
1601 John Bird and Ralph Northey
1602 William Turner and Robert Wade
1603 Thomas Hazlewood and Richard Simnell
1604 Martin Bessell and Thomas Heckford
1605 Henry Osborne and Nicholas Clere
1606 John Bird and Ralph Northey
1607 Thomas Hazlewood and William Mott
1608 Thomas Hazlewood and Thomas Thurston
1609 Robert Wade and John Eldred
1610 Martin Bessell and Nicholas Clere
1611 Thomas Heckford and William Turner
1612 Henry Osborne and Robert Talcott
1613 Thomas Thurston and John Cox
1614 William Turner and William Mott
1615 Thomas Hazlewood and John Marshall
1616 Thomas Thurston and William Hall
1617 John Cox and Henry Barrington
1618 William Turner and Robert Talcott
1619 Martin Bessell and John Marshall
1620 Thomas Heckford and John Norton
1621 William Mott and Thomas Thurston
1622 Robert Talcott and John Cox
1623 John Eldred and Geoffrey Langley
1624 John Marshall and John Norton
1625 Sigismund Sewell and Daniel Cole
1626 Robert Talcott and John Badcock
1627 William Mott and Francis Burrows
1628 Daniel Cole and William Johnson
1629 John Marshall and Henry Barrington
1630 John Norton and Thomas Wade
1631 Robert Talcott and Sigismund Sewell
1632 John Badcock and Robert Buxton
1633 Thomas Wade and John Langley
1634 Daniel Cole and Ralph Harrison

Mayors 1635 - 1713

1635 Daniel Cole
1636 Robert Buxton
1637 Henry Barrington
1638 John Furley
1639 John Langley
1640 Robert Talcott (died in office, succeeded by Henry Barrington)
1641 Thomas Wade
1642 Ralph Harrison
1643 Thomas Laurence
1644 John Cox
1645 Robert Buxton
1646 John Langley
1647 William Cooke
1648 Henry Barrington
1649 Thomas Wade
1650 John Furley
1651 Richard Green
1652 John Radhams
1653 Thomas Peek
1654 Thomas Reynolds
1655 John Radhams elected, but apparently did not serve. Thomas Reynolds continued in office until replaced by Thomas Laurence in December.[63]
1656 John Vickers
1657 Nicholas Beacon
1658 Henry Barrington (replaced by John Radhams)[64]
1659 Thomas Peek
1660 John Gale
1661 John Milbank (replaced by Henry Lamb)
1662 Thomas Reynolds
1663 William Moore
1664 Thomas Wade
1665 Thomas Talcott
1666 William Flanner
1667 Andrew Fromanteel
1668 Ralph Creffield
1669 Henry Lamb
1670 William Moore
1671 John Rayner
1672 Nathaniel Laurence
1673 Ralph Creffield
1674 Henry Lamb
1675 Alexander Hindmarsh
1676 Thomas Green
1677 Ralph Creffield
1678 John Rayner
1679 Nathaniel Laurence
1680 Ralph Creffield
1681 William Moore
1682 Thomas Green
1683 Nathaniel Laurence
1684 John Stilman
1685 William Flanner
1686 Samuel Mott
1687 Alexander Hindmarsh (replaced by John Milbank)[66]
1688 John Milbank
1689 John Potter
1690 Benjamin Cock
1691 John Seabrook
1692 John Stilman
1693 Samuel Mott
1694 Wiliam Moore
1695 John Bacon (died in office, succeeded by John Seabrook)

1696 Nathaniel Laurence the younger
1697 Ralph Creffield the younger
1698 William Boys
1699 William Francis
1700 John Potter
1701 Samuel Featherstone
1702 Ralph Creffield the younger
1703 Samuel Angier
1704 Nathaniel Laurence the younger
1705 John Rainham

1706 James Laurence
1707 George Clark
1708 John Pepper (died in office, succeeded by
   Nathaniel Laurence the elder)
1709 Samuel Angier
1710 Nathaniel Laurence the younger
1711 James Laurence
1712 Peter Johnson
1713 James Laurence
1714 George Clark

A COLCHESTER BAY SEAL, 1618
showing the borough arms on one side
and the castle on the other

THE VICTORIA HISTORY OF THE COUNTY OF ESSEX

The *Victoria History of the County of Essex* forms part of the national series entitled *The Victoria History of the Counties of England* (popularly known as the V.C.H.). The series, which was named after Queen Victoria, was founded in 1899 with the object of compiling a comprehensive work of reference for the history of the English counties on a basis of original research. Each county's history was planned to include 'general' volumes, covering topics (such as archaeology, Domesday Book, administrative, ecclesiastical, and social and economic history) that are best treated on a county-wide basis, and 'topographical' volumes, giving the individual histories of every town and parish in the county. The Victoria History suffered in its early years from the lack of a secure financial basis, but its continuation and expansion were made possible by its acquisition by London University in 1933, and since the 1940s by the involvement of local government authorities in the financing of the project. Over 200 volumes have now been published and 14 county sets completed. Work on another 13 counties, including Essex, is in progress.

Two Essex volumes, vol. I (1903) and II (1907), were published in the early days of the V.C.H. Work on the county resumed in 1951 when the local authorities in the county entered into an agreement with London University to provide the money to complete the Essex set, and a county editor and staff were appointed. In 1977 the County Council, which had for many years been giving practical help, took over from the District Councils the payment of contributions for the administrative county, which had been reduced in size by the creation of the London Boroughs of Barking, Havering, Newham, Redbridge, and Waltham Forest in 1965. The Essex V.C.H. is managed by a committee composed of Essex historians and representatives of the contributing local authorities. Since 1951 one general volume and 6 topographical volumes have been published, in addition to 2 bibliographical volumes.

VOLUME ONE   Natural History, Archaeology, and Domesday Book (1903)

VOLUME TWO   Ecclesiastical, Political, and Economic History (1907)

VOLUME THREE   Roman Essex (1963)

VOLUME FOUR   Ongar Hundred (1956)

VOLUME FIVE   Waltham Hundred, Becontree Hundred (part) (1966)

VOLUME SIX   Becontree Hundred (part), including Newham (1973)

VOLUME SEVEN   Havering-atte-Bower Liberty, Chafford Hundred (part) (1979)

VOLUME EIGHT   Chafford Hundred (part), Harlow Hundred (1983)

VOLUME NINE   Colchester Borough (1994)

BIBLIOGRAPHY (1959)

BIBLIOGRAPHY SUPPLEMENT (1987)

The **Victoria County History of Essex Appeal Fund** (registered charity no. 103880) was set up in 1994. Its aim is to raise additional funds for the Essex V.C.H. at a time when local government funding is threatened by cut-backs in local authority budgets. It is managed by a committee of persons involved and experienced in local history, elected annually at a meeting of the contributors. For further information please contact the Chairman, c/o 70 Duke Street, Chelmsford CM1 1JP.